D1036414

STARTING WITH WITTGENSTEIN

Continuum's *Starting with ...* series offers clear, concise and accessible introductions to the key thinkers in philosophy. The books explore and illuminate the roots of each philosopher's work and ideas, leading readers to a thorough understanding of the key influences and philosophical foundations from which his or her thought developed. Ideal for first-year students starting out in philosophy, the series will serve as the ideal companion to study of this fascinating subject.

Available now:

Starting with Berkeley, Nick Jones

Starting with Derrida, Sean Gaston

Starting with Descartes, C. G. Prado

Starting with Hegel, Craig B. Matarrese

Starting with Heidegger, Tom Greaves

Starting with Hobbes, George MacDonald Ross

Starting with Leibniz, Roger Woolhouse

Starting with Locke, Greg Forster

Starting with Mill, John R. Fitzpatrick

Starting with Nietzsche, Ullrich Haase

Starting with Rousseau, James Delaney

Starting with Sartre, Gail Linsenbard

Forthcoming:

Starting with Hume, Charlotte R. Brown and
     William Edward Morris

Starting with Kant, Andrew Ward

Starting with Kierkegaard, Patrick Sheil

Starting with Merleau-Ponty, Katherine Morris

STARTING WITH WITTGENSTEIN

CHON TEJEDOR

continuum

Continuum International Publishing Group

The Tower Building   80 Maiden Lane
11 York Road   Suite 704
London SE1 7NX   New York, NY 10038

www.continuumbooks.com

British Library Cataloguing-in-Publication Data
A catalogue record for this book is available from the British Library.

ISBN: HB: 978-1-8470-6141-6
PB: 978-1-8470-6142-3

Library of Congress Cataloging-in-Publication Data
Tejedor, Chon.
Starting with Wittgenstein/Chon Tejedor.
p. cm.
ISBN 978-1-84706-141-6 – ISBN 978-1-84706-142-3
1. Wittgenstein, Ludwig, 1889–1951. I. Title.

B3376.W564T42 2011
192–dc22

2010023062

Typeset by RefineCatch Limited, Bungay, Suffolk
Printed and bound in India by Replika Press Pvt Ltd

This book is dedicated to my parents, Ernesto Tejedor and Asución Palau.

CONTENTS

ACKNOWLEDGEMENTS

I would like to thank those colleagues and friends whose conversations over the years have helped shape my views on Wittgenstein, in particular Malcolm Budd, Adrian Moore, Vicente Sanfélix, Alan Thomas, Marie McGinn, Carlos Moya, Luigi Perissinotto, Peter Sullivan, Brian McGuinness, Bill Child, Roger Teichmann, John Hyman, Chris Timpson, Danièle Moyal-Sharrock, John Preston, José Zalabardo, Ian Proops, James Levine, Warren Goldfarb and Dawn Phillips.

I would also like to thank Heather and Roger Burt, for their invaluable practical help in the months prior to the completion of this book and for their on-going support.

Special thanks go to Guy Burt, my long-suffering best friend and husband, without whose help, support and intelligence this book would not have been possible.

This book was written while I was a member of the research project 'Cultura y religión: Wittgenstein y la contra-ilustración' (FFI2008-0086), supported by Spain's Ministry of Science and Innovation.

INTRODUCTION

In many ways, Ludwig Wittgenstein's life story is extraordinary – almost the stuff of legend. He was born in 1889 into one of the richest families in Vienna at the height of Habsburg Empire, and could clearly have devoted himself to a life of luxury. But the thought of relaxing into inherited wealth sat badly with young Wittgenstein, and he set about discovering his calling with a single-minded determination that was to characterize his whole life and work. He tried studying aeronautical engineering for a while before realizing that his true interest lay elsewhere. He threw in aeronautics at the age of twenty-two to travel to Cambridge, drawn there by a newly found passion for philosophy.

It was in Cambridge that he met and was taken on by Bertrand Russell, a don at Trinity College and one of the leading lights of the philosophy of mathematics and logic. Within a year, in spite of the lack of any formal philosophical training, Wittgenstein went from being a stranger to Cambridge and to philosophy, to being singled out as Russell's favourite student, and then to being recognized by one and all as Russell's natural successor. Russell hoped that this unlikely student with his astonishing mind would finish the work he himself was, by that stage, finding too difficult to complete. From nowhere, Wittgenstein established himself in hardly any time at all as a philosopher to watch.

In 1914 World War I broke out and Wittgenstein enlisted as a volunteer in the Austro-Hungarian army. Not even the war could get in the way of what was, by now, an overriding fascination with philosophy. While other men were driven to write poetry in the trenches, Wittgenstein was driven to write philosophy, and it was while fighting at the front that he carried out most of the work that would go towards his first major philosophical book, the *Tractatus Logico-Philosophicus* (TLP). Wittgenstein was a soldier for five years, towards the end of which he was promoted to officer in recognition of his many acts of bravery.

The period that marked Wittgenstein's return to civilian life in 1919 was one of great difficulty and suffering for him. There were any number of obstacles to the publication of the *Tractatus* – not even Wittgenstein's mentor, Russell, could entirely understand the book and the publishers he approached were left stunned with incomprehension. The only point on which there seemed to be a consensus was that the book was impenetrably difficult, unlikely to find an audience, and hence unlikely to sell or make anyone any money. It took four years and a great deal of determination to see the *Tractatus* into print: it was finally published in 1922. The purpose of the book, as Wittgenstein saw it, was to reveal the great issues and problems that had dogged philosophers for centuries as being essentially shams: mistakes of understanding which could be dissolved by clarifying the language and the concepts in which they were couched. In carrying out this task of clarification, Wittgenstein saw the *Tractatus* as effectively signalling the end of traditional philosophy in its entirety. The great centuries-old debates were really just the story of the Emperor's new clothes writ large; the *Tractatus* would be the lone voice crying out the truth . . . if anyone would ever read it, or understand it.

It was not only the scepticism of publishers and the incomprehension of other philosophers that impacted on Wittgenstein after the war. In the summer of 1918, he had heard of the death of his long-term partner, David Pinsent, who had been a student with him in Cambridge before the war. David had died the previous May in an aeroplane accident in the United Kingdom, while engaged in engineering research into aerodynamics – much the field that Wittgenstein had abandoned in his early twenties.

When Wittgenstein finally returned to defeated Vienna, having spent several months in prisoner of war camps in Italy, he abandoned his philosophical work. Instead of returning to Cambridge, he gave away his share of the considerable family inheritance and set out to work first as a gardener at the Klosterneuburg Monastery and then as a primary school teacher in the small rural village of Trattenbach. David's death had struck him very severely, and his decision to abandon Cambridge and remain in Austria was probably the result as much of grief as of the conviction that the *Tractatus* – which he would dedicate to David – had in any case resolved all the problems of philosophy, thereby at a stroke rendering the Cambridge philosophy scene and indeed philosophy in general obsolete and redundant.

For long enough Wittgenstein really did seem to have believed that there was no more genuine work to be done in the field of philosophy: he had grappled with it in the trenches, discovered its weaknesses, and laid them bare. There was certainly no reason for him to return to Cambridge. By the end of the 1920s, though, the situation had started to alter. Wittgenstein had been drawn back into thinking about philosophy through his (initially reluctant) involvement with the members of the philosophical group called the Vienna Circle. Furthermore, and perhaps to his publisher's surprise, the *Tractatus* was being read; more than that, it was attracting much attention in the philosophical world and gaining many devoted followers. There was suddenly an upsurge of interest in this new brand of philosophy. People were starting to take it seriously.

Just as other people were starting to get to grips with his work, though, Wittgenstein himself was becoming dissatisfied with it and was taking the first steps along a road which would eventually lead to him returning to Cambridge, there to dismantle the logic of the *Tractatus* entirely. In its place he would propose an entirely new philosophical method – one that would crystallize in the book *Philosophical Investigations* (PI). Although this process was already underway when he came back to Cambridge in 1929, Wittgenstein remained, at that point, sufficiently persuaded by his earlier book to present it at his doctoral thesis.

Getting a doctorate was a necessary, though at the same time quite farcical, process for Wittgenstein. His examiners were G. E. Moore and Bertrand Russell. Russell, amused by the idea of having to examine someone he had come to regard as his philosophical equal (if not superior), commented to Moore: 'I have never known anything so absurd in my whole life.' Moore himself wrote rather jokingly in the examiners' report: 'It is my personal opinion that Mr Wittgenstein's thesis is a work of genius; but, be that as it may, it is certainly well up to the standard required for the Cambridge degree of Doctor of Philosophy.'[1] Work of genius notwithstanding, Wittgenstein's doctorate enabled him to remain in Cambridge, where he was awarded a series of research and lecturing positions. He never returned to gardening or primary-school teaching.

During the years that followed, he would have three more close personal relationships – with Marguerite Respinger, whom he considered marrying, with Francis Skinner and with Ben Richards. By the time he was elected professor, in 1939, he was widely acknowledged to be the major philosophical figure of his time, as is made abundantly clear by the remark from C. D. Broad: 'To refuse the chair to Wittgenstein would be like refusing Einstein a chair of physics'.[2] Wittgenstein continued working until his death in 1951, writing the last entry in what would become his last philosophical work (*On Certainty*) the day before consciousness finally slipped from him.

There is no doubt that Wittgenstein's contribution to philosophy is extraordinary. He pioneered at least two altogether distinct philosophical methods: one encapsulated in his *Tractatus Logico-Philosophicus*; the other culminating in the *Philosophical Investigations*. Both of these works were – and remain – in many ways revolutionary. But the publishers who rejected the *Tractatus* when Wittgenstein was still a young man had a point: his work certainly can seem impenetrably difficult at times. Even the matter of interpreting exactly what his books mean has been a matter of contention and energized debate for many years.

The aim of this book, then, is to take the reader through admittedly difficult territory in as clear a manner as possible. We will be looking at the major themes in Wittgenstein's earlier and later philosophies: in Part I we will focus on the *Tractatus* and its views on language, the mind and ethics, while in Part II we will tackle Wittgenstein's later views on meaning, rules and sensations. The territory we are crossing will at times be difficult, but like many difficult journeys it will also be rewarding – even beautiful.

PART I

THE EARLIER WITTGENSTEIN

CHAPTER 1

LANGUAGE AND LOGIC

i. INTRODUCTION

In this section, we will begin our examination of Wittgenstein's earlier discussion of language. Some aspects of Wittgenstein's discussion can be rather subtle and complex, others can be quite technical. The ground we are about to cover is generally recognized among philosophers as being particularly challenging, and most people find that they need to return to the concepts several times before they feel properly familiar with them. This experience is very common and is widely acknowledged by those who study the *Tractatus* (there should really be some kind of survivors' help group for this material!). So although, at times, it can be a frustrating experience, it is also an enormously rewarding one.

In this chapter, then, we will be focusing primarily on Wittgenstein's notions of the sentence and of the proposition, on his understanding of logical analysis and on his use of truth-tables. In so doing, we will be laying down notions that are of fundamental importance to our later understanding of some of Wittgenstein's most intriguing insights: insights on the pictoriality of propositions and thoughts, on the self, on ethics, and, ultimately, on the status of the *Tractatus* itself.

ii. SENTENCES AND PROPOSITIONS

Perhaps the best place to start our investigation of Wittgenstein's views on language is with his notions of the sentence and of the proposition. Wittgenstein uses these terms in a very strict, technical way that does not always coincide with the way in which we might ordinarily use them, so our first task will be to clarify what he means by them. Wittgenstein uses the term 'sentence' (which he also sometimes calls 'propositional sign') to refer to a specific arrangement of words. For instance, the sentence 'The earth revolves around the sun' is an arrangement in which the word 'earth' comes before the word 'revolves', the word 'revolves' comes before the word 'sun', and so on. Sentences like this can occur in a variety of media. The sentences that make up this book, for example, consist of words printed in black ink on white paper. If I were presenting this book in a series of lectures, however, I would do so by means of spoken – not written – words: the sentences in my lectures would be arrangements of spoken words. In turn, if this book was in Braille, the sentences would be arrangements of raised dots.

Sentences, then, are arrangements of words that can belong to different media; and for Wittgenstein, sentences have two central characteristics. The first characteristic – one that is shared in common by sentences in all media – is that the words that make them up can be perceived through the senses: the printed words in this book can be perceived through the sense of sight; the spoken words in a lecture can be perceived through the sense of hearing; words in Braille can be perceived through the sense of touch, etc. So, for Wittgenstein, sentences are arrangements of words that belong to different media and that can be perceived through the senses.

The second characteristic of sentences, in his view, is this: sentences can be used to make statements about *possible ways in which reality could be* – or, as Wittgenstein puts it, about 'possible states'. The notion of possible states is right at the heart of Wittgenstein's thinking about language and we will be coming back to examine it more fully later in this chapter. For now, I will only consider those aspects of the notion of possible state that help to give an initial approximation to how they relate to sentences, in Wittgenstein's view.

A possible state is a possible way in which reality could be. It is something that could either occur or not occur in reality. It is a *possibility*: something that could happen to be the case, but that could also happen not to be the case. A rubber ball being blue all over could be an example of a possible state: it is certainly possible that a rubber ball be blue, and it is equally possible that it be (say) red and white striped instead. Even if we are holding the ball in our hands and can see that it is, in fact, blue all over, we can reasonably imagine it being other colours; those are clear possibilities that *could* have existed, although the ball being blue is the possibility that actually *obtains*. Sentences – i.e. arrangements of words – can be used to make statements about possible states, statements about the possible ways in which reality could be. 'The ball is blue all over' and 'The ball is red and white striped' are both sentences.

But Wittgenstein goes further than this. He suggests that one and the same sentence – one and the same specific arrangement of words – can be used to make a *variety* of statements about possible states of reality. Consider, for instance, the sentence: 'The bald eagle expert is on the television'. This arrangement of words (where the word 'The' comes first, then the word 'bald', then the word 'eagle', and so forth) can be used to make a statement about an expert in bald eagles – but it can also be used to make a statement about an expert in eagles who happens to be bald. This expert – bald or hirsute – may be appearing in a television transmission that we are watching, or, if he is the athletic type, he could conceivably be balancing on top of the television in our living room – literally 'on' the television. And there are further options here. For instance, if we were secret agents speaking in code, we might use this sentence (this particular arrangement of words) to make a very different statement: perhaps a statement relating to the safe arrival of some secret parcel. The sentence 'The bald eagle expert is on the television' can therefore be used to make at least five different statements: two relating to an expert in bald eagles (either literally or figuratively 'on' the television), another two relating to an expert in eagles who happens to be bald (again, either in a programme or balanced on the device), and another one relating, not to eagles and experts at all, but to a secret agent's parcel.

This is already quite a bewildering variety for what appeared on first sight to be a relatively simple sentence – and according to Wittgenstein, all sentences are like this. Every sentence (every arrangement of words) is such that it can be used to make a variety of statements about possible ways in which reality could be. Consider another example: the sentence 'The elephant is dying'. This arrangement of words can be used to make a statement about an elephant; but it can also be used to make a statement about a boxer nicknamed 'the elephant'. The word 'dying' might be meant literally or figuratively: the pachyderm might be coming to the end of its life or the boxer might be losing a fight. And so on, and so on. The key idea here is that while a given sentence is a fixed arrangement of words, that fixed arrangement may give rise to a wide variety of statements about the possible ways in which reality might be.

So sentences can be used to make a variety of statements about possible states – and this is the manner in which we encounter sentences in our everyday lives. Generally, we make an educated judgement about what statement a given sentence is intended to express (out of the various statements it *could* express). This is how we manage to communicate everyday. But a question that arises at this point is: how do we come to make the decision as to *which* statement a sentence is intended to express? In other words, what is involved in making the educated judgement that a sentence expresses one particular statement, rather than the various others it could be expressing? Wittgenstein says surprisingly little on this clearly important issue in the *Tractatus*. There are two main reasons for his reluctance to discuss it in more detail. The first has to do with the idea that this question, when understood in a particular way, is one for psychology – not philosophy – to answer. The second reason is that, when the question is understood in a more philosophical manner, it turns out that it cannot actually be discussed as such in any detail. We will consider these ideas in the conclusion to Part I. In this chapter, I will give an initial overview of Wittgenstein's (limited) discussion of this and other related questions. If, by the end of this chapter, you are left feeling that not enough has been said on these matters, be reassured that there are reasons for Wittgenstein's circumspection – reasons we will be considering later on.

As we saw before, Wittgenstein suggests in the *Tractatus* that a sentence is an arrangement of words that can be used to make a variety of statements. When a sentence is used to make one very specific statement about a particular possible state, Wittgenstein calls it a *proposition*. In other words, a proposition is a sentence that is used to affirm one specific possible state of reality: it is an arrangement of words that is used to make a specific statement about a specific, possible way in which reality could be. The distinction between a sentence and a proposition is illustrated in the following remark, as well as others:[3]

> In order to recognise a [proposition] by its [sentence] we must observe how it is used with a sense. (TLP 3.326)

For Wittgenstein, a sentence becomes a proposition when it is *used* to make one specific statement out of the various ones it could be making. And we recognize which proposition (which statement) a sentence expresses by observing *how* the sentence is used. Let us consider an example here. We saw above that the sentence 'The bald eagle expert is on the television' (this arrangement of words) can be used to make at least five different statements. This can also be put by saying that the sentence can be used to *express* five different *propositions* about five different possible states. How do we recognize which of these propositions the sentence expresses at any one time? According to Wittgenstein, by observing how the sentence is being used. If the sentence is used as part of a discussion of a television programme on bald eagles, we will take it in one way. If it is used as part of a discussion of our house guest, the expert on eagles who happens to be bald and who has recently lost his mind and taken to climbing on the appliances, we will take it in another way. If it is used in a conversation between secret agents, we will take it in yet another way. We *recognize* which proposition the sentence expresses by considering how it is being used. At the level of the sentence, the sentence expresses one proposition in particular when it is used in one particular way.

We can see, then, that for Wittgenstein, the distinction between sentences and propositions is absolutely vital, and we will need to bear it constantly in mind if we are to follow his thinking on the internal structure of language. In what follows, I will always make it clear whether I am referring to a sentence (i.e. to an arrangement of words) or to a proposition (a specific statement) expressed by a sentence. So, I might say, for example: the sentence 'The bald eagle expert is on the television' – thereby signalling that I am referring to this arrangement of words, to this sentence that could be used to express a variety of propositions (rather than to any specific one of those propositions). If, on the other hand, I wish to pick out one specific proposition expressed by the sentence, I will explain how the sentence is being used and I will then say: the proposition '. . .'; or the proposition expressed by the sentence '. . .' – thereby signalling that I intend to pick out one particular statement.

For Wittgenstein, propositions are specific statements about reality: they affirm – or 'represent', as he sometimes puts it – specific possible states. These statements can be true or false. A proposition is true when the possible state it represents obtains in reality. Let us imagine that, as part of an astronomy lesson, the teacher says: 'It might look to us like the sun revolves around the earth; in fact, however, the earth revolves around the sun'. Here, the sentences 'the sun revolves around the earth' and 'the earth revolves around the sun' are used to express two different propositions about the relative movements of the planet earth and the sun. The proposition expressed by 'the earth revolves around the sun' is true: it represents a possible state that obtains, as a fact, in reality. In contrast, the proposition expressed by 'the sun revolves around the earth' is false. This proposition represents a *possible* state of reality; for it is possible that the sun should, in reality, have revolved around the earth. (Admittedly this would only be possible in a universe with rather different laws of gravity and motion, but it is nevertheless *conceivable*, and as such *possible*.) It is just that this possibility of the sun revolving around the earth is not realized as a fact, it does not obtain in our universe: the proposition is therefore false. Wittgenstein would say that both of these propositions have a 'sense' – by which he means that each of them represents a particular *possible* state of reality. It is just that, given what happens to obtain in reality, the former is true and the latter is false.

For Wittgenstein, it is an essential feature of propositions that they should be '*determinately* either true or false'. By this he means that there must be an absolutely precise answer to the question of whether a proposition is true or false. This does not mean that we can necessarily find out the answer ourselves – our intellectual powers or the information we have at hand may not stretch so far as to enable us to do so. Nevertheless, the proposition will be determinately either one or the other: it will either represent something that obtains in reality or not – there can be no grey areas in this respect. Consider again the proposition expressed by 'The earth revolves around the sun' in the above example. Until the sixteenth Century, this proposition was thought by many to be false; in fact, however, the proposition is true – and it was true even before Copernicus demonstrated it to be true. Indeed it was, and always has been, *determinately* true, irrespective of whether our ancestors knew it to be true at the time.

So, in Wittgenstein's view, there must be an absolutely precise answer to the question of whether a proposition is true or false, even if we do not know what the answer to it is. This means in particular that propositions are never both true and false. Similarly, propositions are never neither true nor false. They are always one or the other. If a string of words appears to be both true and false, or if it appears to be neither true nor false, then Wittgenstein would suggest it is simply not a proposition. Perhaps the string of words is not being used in a precise enough manner, perhaps it is not being used to make the kind of specific statement that counts as a proposition. At any rate, if an arrangement of words is used to affirm a specific possible state, then the result will be a proposition that will be determinately either true or false in these three respects: there will be a precise answer to the question of whether it is true or false; it will not be both true and false; and it will not be such as to be neither true nor false. Wittgenstein sometimes puts this by saying that the proposition will have a determinate truth-value.

> A proposition *shows* how things stand *if* it is true. And it *says that* they do so stand. (TLP 4.022)

> A proposition must restrict reality to two alternatives: yes or no. (TLP 4.023)

The idea that propositions are determinately true or false in this respect is sometimes put by saying that propositions are 'bivalent'. In addition, Wittgenstein suggests that propositions are also 'bipolar'. Propositions are bipolar in that they are *both* capable of being true and capable of being false. The idea is that propositions have to be bipolar because they set out to be informative about the world. That propositions set out to be informative is part and parcel of the concept of proposition: a proposition affirms a possible way in which reality might be – in this respect, it sets out to convey information about reality. (When the proposition is true, the information is correct; when it is false, it isn't.) The connection between the bipolarity of propositions and their being informative is made clearer if we consider the expression 'either it is raining or it is not raining'. 'Either it is raining or it is not raining' is not bipolar. It is not *capable* of being false: it is true when it is raining and it is also true when it is not raining – in other words, it is true under all circumstances, there are no circumstances under which it is false. As a result, it tells us nothing about the world: in particular, it conveys no information about the state of the weather. For a proposition to be informative, it needs to be bipolar: it needs to depict a possibility that could genuinely either obtain or not obtain. 'It is raining or it is not raining' is not, therefore, a genuine proposition. 'It is raining' and 'It is not raining', on the other hand, are.

In Summary

– A sentence is an arrangement of words that can be used to make a variety of statements about possible states (about possible ways in which reality could be).
– These statements about possible states are called propositions.
– A proposition is a sentence that is used to make a specific statement about a particular possible state. When a sentence is used to make such a statement, it expresses a proposition.
– A proposition is determinately either true or false: it has a determinate truth-value. It is true when the possibility it represents obtains in reality and false when it does not.
– The sense of the proposition is the possible state represented by that proposition.

iii. ESSENTIAL AND ACCIDENTAL FEATURES OF PROPOSITIONS

According to Wittgenstein, that propositions should be determinately either true or false is an essential feature of propositions. Something is simply not a proposition if it is not determinately either true or false. That a proposition should possess a determinate truth-value is part and parcel of the very concept of proposition.

But Wittgenstein suggests that propositions have accidental features as well as essential ones. The essential features of propositions are those without which they would simply not be propositions. The accidental features of a proposition, in contrast, are those features that the proposition possesses, but which it could fail to possess without ceasing to be a proposition. A parallel can be drawn here with the concept of bachelor: the concept of bachelor is such that a bachelor can have blond hair, but can also fail to have blond hair (or, indeed, any hair!) without ceasing to be a bachelor. In contrast, a bachelor cannot fail to be unmarried without ceasing to be a bachelor. Having blond hair is an accidental feature of bachelors; being unmarried is an essential feature of bachelors. (The parallel I have just drawn between the concept of bachelor and that of the proposition should be taken with a pinch of salt. The analogy is problematic in important ways, but it is also helpful for illustrative purposes. I will return to this issue in the conclusion to Part I.)

In Wittgenstein's view, the accidental features of propositions arise primarily from the fact that propositions are expressed by means of words and sentences that belong to 'natural languages'. By a 'natural language', Wittgenstein means here one of the languages employed in everyday life, such as English and Spanish – everyday language, in other words, of the kind that has developed naturally to serve the pragmatic ends of communication, our survival and the survival of our communities. Wittgenstein notes that two propositions, expressed by means of two different sentences in different languages, can have the same sense: they can represent the same possible state of reality. Imagine that two school friends are discussing the marital status of their teachers and that these friends are both bilingual, so much so that sometimes they say things in English and sometimes in Spanish. Now, imagine that, as part of this conversation, they use the sentences 'Ivan is a bachelor' and 'Ivan está soltero' to represent the same possible state. In Wittgenstein's view, we have two propositions here: one expressed by the English-language sentence 'Ivan is a bachelor' and another expressed by the Spanish-language sentence 'Ivan está soltero'. Both propositions have the same sense, however; they represent the same possible state. These are two different propositions in that they are expressed by means of different sentences; but they have the same sense in that they represent the same possibility, the same possible way in which reality could be. So, two propositions belonging to two different natural languages can have the same sense: they can affirm the same possible state of reality by means of different words and sentences. This suggests that neither the English-language words ('is', 'bachelor', etc.) nor the Spanish-language ones ('está', 'soltero', etc.) are essential to the expression of that particular sense. The possible state in question can be represented equally well in either language: it is not essential that it should be represented in one or other of the two. That the former proposition is expressed by means of English-language words and the latter by means of Spanish-language ones is incidental to their being propositions with a sense: it is an accidental feature of these propositions. In contrast, that these propositions should be determinately either true or false is an essential feature of them. Something can be a proposition without it being expressed in English or Spanish; but it cannot be a proposition if it is not determinately either true or false. The distinction between the essential and the accidental features of a proposition emerges in the following remark:

A proposition possesses essential and accidental features.

Accidental features are those that result from the particular way in which the propositional sign [the sentence] is produced. Essential features are those without which the proposition could not express its sense. (TLP 3.34)

In Summary

– Propositions have essential features, without which they would simply not be propositions. Being determinately either true or false is an essential feature of propositions.
– Propositions also have accidental features, which they can lack without ceasing to be propositions. Being expressed by means of words belonging to natural languages is an accidental feature of propositions.

iv. LOGICAL ANALYSIS

So far, then, we have seen that two propositions (such as those expressed in the above example by 'Ivan is a bachelor' and 'Ivan está soltero') can have the same sense even though they possess different accidental features – i.e. even though they are expressed by means of words and sentences belonging to different natural languages. Wittgenstein thought that, for this to be possible, propositions such as these must share something in common: something about these propositions must be essentially the same, in spite of their obvious differences, if they are to have the same sense. What can propositions such as these have in common, however? Clearly it cannot be anything to do with the words with which they are expressed, since these words are different in each case. So is there, somehow, something underlying the words of natural language that fixes the sense of the proposition? It is partly in order to address this question that Wittgenstein introduces another of the central notions of the *Tractatus*: the notion of logical analysis.

In the *Tractatus*, Wittgenstein holds that propositions in natural languages can undergo a process he calls 'logical analysis'. Ordinary propositions can be logically analyzed; they can be broken down into further propositions. Consider, for instance, the proposition 'Ivan is a bachelor' in the above example. If we were to analyze this proposition logically, we might begin by breaking it up into further propositions – say the propositions 'Ivan is a man' and 'Ivan is not married'. Each of these two propositions could, in turn, be further analyzed: for instance, 'Ivan is a man' could be further analyzed into 'Ivan is a human being' and 'Ivan is male', etc.

Logical analysis is an important philosophical tool, according to the *Tractatus*. One of its central purposes is that of clarifying the sense of propositions. Imagine that you were unsure as to the sense of the proposition 'Ivan is a bachelor' – for instance, because you did not know what a bachelor was. Logical analysis would enable you clarify the sense of this proposition by making it clear that a bachelor is a man who is not married. Logical analysis helps to clarify sense: as the logical analysis of a proposition progresses, the precise sense of that proposition becomes increasingly clear. Logical analysis, then, is a philosophical tool for the clarification of sense, whereby each step of the analysis yields a more basic, more precise statement.

Wittgenstein suggests that the logical analysis of any given proposition eventually comes to a clear and determinate stopping point – a point where the resultant propositions are themselves not capable of being broken down into any further constituent propositions. When a proposition has been analyzed all the way to this stopping point, it is said to have been 'completely analyzed'. This notion of complete analysis is at the heart of Wittgenstein's understanding of the proposition. Because (as we have seen) propositions are rigidly logical in their structure and behaviour, Wittgenstein argues that every proposition has one and only one complete logical analysis: there is one and only one correct complete analysis for any given proposition.

It is this notion of logical analysis which proceeds to a stopping point that explains, rather elegantly, what two propositions with the same sense (such as the English-language proposition 'Ivan is a bachelor' and the Spanish-language proposition 'Ivan está soltero') have in common despite their obvious differences. Wittgenstein says that if two propositions have the same sense, their logical analyses must, ultimately, coincide. That is, although the first steps of their logical analyses might differ (through being expressed in different natural languages), at the deepest level of analysis, when their analyses come to the stopping point, the two propositions will yield the same results. By having in the final analysis the same constituent propositions as their foundation, two seemingly dissimilar surface-level propositions can share the same sense.

Let us take a closer look at how this works by considering again the propositions 'Ivan is a bachelor' and 'Ivan está soltero'. The first steps in the analyses of these propositions yield different results: 'Ivan is a bachelor' initially breaks down into further English-language propositions ('Ivan is a man' and 'Ivan is not married'); 'Ivan está soltero', in contrast, initially breaks down into Spanish-language propositions ('Ivan es un hombre' and 'Ivan no está casado'). According to Wittgenstein, however, if we were to continue the analyses of these propositions – a process that might take a very long time! – we would find that, ultimately, the propositions that emerge from them become increasingly precise. More importantly, by the time one reaches the ultimate steps of analysis, one is no longer working with propositions in natural languages at all. Instead one is working at a highly rarefied, purely logical level, in which language loses all of its accidental features and retains only those which are essential to the expression of sense. Hence, the propositions that arise at the ultimate level of analysis no longer belong to any specific natural language: they belong to a highly refined and precise logical language that encompasses only what is essential. So the process of logical analysis ultimately strips propositions of the accidental features characteristic of natural languages, and transforms them into absolutely unambiguous propositions.

You may be thinking that it would be useful here to have an example of a proposition that has been analyzed to this ultimate level, or indeed perhaps a short primer of the 'logical language' that expresses things with such precision and clarity. Unfortunately we do not have such an example – Wittgenstein does not give any, for reasons which we will go into in the next section. For now, all we need to bear in mind is that the idea of analyzing propositions down to a stopping point of logical unambiguity was crucial to Wittgenstein. We may look upon this process of logical analysis, rather as we take on trust the notion of subatomic particles like quarks, although we have ourselves never seen them in any conventional sense or been presented with an 'example' of a quark in any everyday context.

Wittgenstein calls the propositions that emerge at the ultimate level of analysis 'elementary propositions', in order to distinguish them from the ordinary, surface level propositions of natural languages. In Section vi, we will consider in more detail Wittgenstein's discussion of 'elementary propositions'. At this stage, let us simply note that the 'elementary propositions' that emerge at the ultimate level of analysis belong to an absolutely precise logical language that comprises only that which is essential to the expression of sense (to the representation of possible states), and that they cannot themselves be analyzed into further propositions. To use our particle analogy again, we might think of surface propositions expressed in natural language as being broadly similar to pieces of matter – things we can perceive with our senses, see and touch in everyday life. But if we analyze them into their constituent parts we will eventually get to molecules, and thence to atoms, and thence to quarks – none of which are touchable or visible, but whose existence we can deduce from the behaviour of the things we can touch and see. Wittgenstein was comfortable that he had made a comparable deduction and that what it pointed to was the existence of elementary propositions.

Wittgenstein suggests that when two ordinary (i.e. non-elementary) propositions – such as 'Ivan is a bachelor' and 'Ivan está soltero' – have the same sense, they can be logically analyzed into the same 'elementary propositions'. This is what that is common to them: this is what enables them to have the same sense in spite of displaying, at the non-analyzed level, different accidental features. Although propositions such as 'Ivan is a bachelor' and 'Ivan está soltero' seem very different at the surface level, their full analyses would – if carried out – reveal that they ultimately break down in the same way: at the ultimate level of analysis, the (accidental) differences between them vanish, and we are left with the same 'elementary propositions'.

For Wittgenstein, all non-elementary propositions, no matter what natural language they are expressed in, are ultimately analyzable into combinations of 'elementary propositions' belonging to one common, purely logical language. Propositions with the same sense ultimately break down into the same combination of 'elementary propositions'; propositions with different senses ultimately break down into different combinations of 'elementary propositions' – just as different materials break down into different arrangements of atoms, while one material (whether it be formed into a drinking glass or a windowpane) ultimately breaks down into the same arrangement of atoms. What is crucial, for Wittgenstein, is that, at the ultimate level of analysis, the propositions that emerge are altogether different from the propositions of natural languages: 'elementary propositions' are couched in a logical language that is absolutely precise. In the next section, we will consider in a little more detail what Wittgenstein understands by this.

In Summary

- Logical analysis is the process of logically breaking down a proposition into increasingly precise and increasingly basic further propositions.
- Logical analysis helps to clarify the sense of propositions.
- Logical analysis comes to a definite stopping point: every proposition has one and only one complete logical analysis to that stopping point.
- At the ultimate level of analysis, the propositions that emerge are no longer propositions of natural languages. They are the absolutely precise and unambiguous propositions of a purely logical language. In order to distinguish them from ordinary, surface-level propositions, Wittgenstein call the propositions that emerge at this ultimate level 'elementary propositions'.
- Two ordinary (i.e. non-elementary) propositions with the same sense – such as 'Ivan is a bachelor' and 'Ivan está soltero' – will ultimately be analyzable into the same combination of 'elementary propositions'.

v. A PURELY LOGICAL LANGUAGE – WITH NO EXAMPLES!

In this section, I would like to consider in a little more detail the issue of why Wittgenstein does not provide us with any examples of elementary propositions. We have seen that, for Wittgenstein, all ordinary propositions of natural languages can be logically analyzed and that their logical analyses eventually come to a determinate stopping point. At this point the propositions that emerge are no longer couched in natural languages: they are 'elementary propositions' and belong to an absolutely precise and unambiguous logical language. As we saw above, we would very much welcome some examples of these 'elementary propositions'. Wittgenstein does not provide any, however. Not only does he offer no examples of 'elementary propositions', but he also admits that he has never even come across any! Indeed, by his own admission, Wittgenstein never carried out the complete analysis of any proposition: he never pursued the logical analysis of any proposition to its ultimate level – to the level where 'elementary propositions' supposedly emerge. Nor did he believe any other logician to have achieved such a feat. Nevertheless, Wittgenstein aims, in the *Tractatus*, to provide us with an insight into what takes place at the ultimate level of analysis even though he has no examples to offer us in this area.

It is possible to draw a series of analogies to help illustrate this point. These analogies are, once again, problematic in several respects (for reasons we will consider in Chapter 2 and in the conclusion to Part I). But I still think they are helpful enough for us to include them here. Consider first the case of a physicist working on subatomic particles. Particle physicists posit invisible, untouchable subatomic particles through careful scrutiny of things that are visible and touchable. We cannot see or touch these particles – they are too small for 'seeing' or 'touching' to be possible – but there is a sense in which we cannot fully understand things at the ordinary, visible, touchable level without them. (Indeed, it is because physicists regard them as essential to their understanding of what takes place at the ordinary level that they end up including them in their models.) In some ways, Wittgenstein sees himself as doing something similar in the *Tractatus*. By considering the workings of ordinary propositions – propositions expressed in sentences that can be seen, heard or touched – he is led to the notion of elementary propositions. He has no examples of elementary propositions to offer us, but he posits them nevertheless, because he regards them as essential to our understanding of what takes at the level of ordinary language.

It might seem rather frustrating not to have concrete examples of elementary propositions to work with. How can we be certain that they are part of language in the way Wittgenstein suggests, if he does not provide us with any concrete examples? Although we may feel this is a problem, Wittgenstein does not, simply because his aim is to clarify the concept of proposition: to increase our understanding of what a proposition is. Let us look, once again, at the analogy to the concept of bachelor. If you understand the concept of 'bachelor' fully, then you already know that it is part and parcel of this concept that a bachelor be unmarried – and you can know this without having been presented with any bachelors in real life. Similarly, Wittgenstein suggests that if we work at fully understanding the concept of a proposition, then we will come to see that it must ultimately be analyzable into elementary propositions which are themselves not analyzable further. That we do not have access to any examples of these elementary propositions should not hinder our ability to acknowledge that they are essential for the concept of the proposition itself to work. No scientist has ever seen a quark – or even an atom! – with their own eyes; but positing them is essential to their understanding of what we can see. Similarly, for Wittgenstein, elementary propositions are essential to our understanding of the ordinary propositions we come across in natural languages. He writes:

It is obvious that the analysis of propositions must bring us to elementary propositions. (TLP 4.221)

In spite of Wittgenstein's claim that this is 'obvious', this is clearly very dense material! Because it is so central to Wittgenstein's view, it is worth going over it carefully, so we are going to look at it step by step. First, we will examine in more detail Wittgenstein's understanding of what takes place at the ultimate level of analysis: his understanding of 'elementary propositions'. This will be the task of Section vi. Then, in Section vii, we will go on to consider in what way, in his view, the notion of 'elementary proposition' is embedded in the broader concept of 'proposition'.

In Summary

- Wittgenstein does not offer any examples of the complete logical analysis of any proposition. He therefore offers no examples of 'elementary propositions'.
- Wittgenstein believes that this lack of examples is not a problem. He believes that it is possible to gain an insight into the ultimate level of analysis (an insight into 'elementary propositions') merely by examining the broader concept of proposition – more specifically, what takes place at the level of ordinary language.
- In Wittgenstein's view, the concept of proposition has built into it that all propositions should ultimately be analyzable into 'elementary propositions' – just like the concept of bachelor has built into it that bachelors are unmarried. This means that, by paying careful attention to the concept of proposition, it is possible to gain an understanding of 'elementary propositions'.

vi. ELEMENTARY PROPOSITIONS AND NAMES; STATES OF AFFAIRS AND OBJECTS

In this section, we are going to examine Wittgenstein's discussion of what takes place at the ultimate level of analysis: his discussion of 'elementary propositions'. Then, in the next section, we will consider why, according to Wittgenstein, it belongs to the concept of proposition that all propositions should be analyzable into 'elementary propositions'.

As we saw before, the 'elementary propositions' that emerge at the ultimate level of analysis are very different from the ordinary propositions of natural languages. Ordinary propositions are expressed by means of words and sentences that are familiar to us and that we recognize easily. Because they are expressed in this way, ordinary propositions may come across as ambiguous, they may be misinterpreted: natural language sentences may have many subtly or widely different meanings, be intended figuratively not literally, and so forth. This is not so in the case of 'elementary propositions'. For 'elementary propositions' do not belong to a natural language that might be familiar to us, such as English or Spanish. Instead, they belong to a highly specialized and precise logical language, one which in incapable of being misinterpreted, one which only ever means one thing at one time, indeed one which we may feel is more like mathematics than language. The 'elementary propositions' of this logical language are arrangements of what Wittgenstein calls 'names'. These 'names' differ from ordinary words in that they are absolutely precise and unambiguous. Part of the reason for this is that, at the fully analyzed level, every 'name' has one and only one meaning. This removes the ambiguities that arise, at the ordinary, non-analyzed level, from the fact that words in natural languages can be used to express a variety of senses. (Think, for instance, of 'The bald eagle expert is on television'.) So, in the logical language that emerges at the fully analyzed level, each 'name' has one and only one meaning – rather in the same way that, in mathematics, '2' always means two, and never seven or nine.

In addition, these 'names' are also special in that, according to Wittgenstein, their meanings are unchangeable, indestructible and simple. 'Unchangeable' and 'indestructible' are clear enough here – the meanings of 'names' cannot change and they cannot be destroyed. The idea that names have meanings that are simple requires some further clarification, however. For Wittgenstein, the meanings of these 'names' are simple, in that they cannot be broken down – or analyzed into – into even simpler meanings. They are the most basic, the most fundamental, building blocks of language, and do not consist of any further, more-rudimentary, structures.

So, names are unchangeable, indestructible and simple. In Wittgenstein's view, there is an intimate relation between these three features of the meanings of 'names'. Specifically, Wittgenstein suggests that the meanings of 'names' are unchangeable and indestructible *because* they are simple. So what, exactly, is the connection between, on the one hand, the simplicity of meaning and, on the other, its inability to change or to be destroyed?

Well, Wittgenstein's thinking seems to have been as follows: things that are built up of parts (i.e. things that are not simple) can change in that their parts can be replaced with others or can be reorganized. We might think here of all the physical objects that we meet in our daily life: any one of them can, with effort, be altered, pulled apart, modified or reordered, by virtue of a basic property of matter – that it is all made up of smaller, more fundamental items (like molecules, and atoms, and quarks). But the 'names' Wittgenstein talks of are not like this. They are themselves the most basic building blocks, incapable of being further broken down. Since the meanings of names do not consist of further meaningful parts (that is what makes them simple) they are incapable of changing. If we accept this reasoning, it also follows that the meanings of 'names' cannot be destroyed in that, being simple, they cannot be disassembled: they do not consist of parts that can be entirely separated. According to Wittgenstein, therefore, it is because the meanings of names are simple that they are unchangeable and indestructible.

Wittgenstein calls the meanings of 'names' 'objects'. An 'object', in the *Tractatus*, is therefore the simple, indestructible and unchangeable meaning of a 'name'. The choice of the term 'object' may seem surprising here. After all, the term 'object' is normally used to refer to those things we come across in everyday life – such as planets and televisions, things which are capable of changing and of being destroyed. In Philosophy, however, there is a very long tradition of using the term 'object' to refer to something totally unlike the things we come across in our everyday lives. An object, in Philosophy, can be something highly abstract, that does not exist or cease to exist in the way that ordinary things do. There is little doubt that Wittgenstein is using the term 'object' in this way, in the *Tractatus*: an 'object', here, is simply the absolutely simple, unchangeable and indestructible meaning of a 'name'.

So, for Wittgenstein, all propositions can ultimately be analyzed into elementary propositions. Elementary propositions are the most basic propositions there can be. They are arrangements of names that have simple, unchangeable and indestructible meanings. Wittgenstein calls the meanings of names objects. Elementary propositions, like all propositions, represent possible ways in which reality could be: they represent possibilities. And since elementary propositions are the most basic of propositions, the possibilities they represent are the most basic of all. Wittgenstein calls these most basic possibilities states of affairs. He suggests that states of affairs – the basic possibilities represented by elementary propositions – are themselves arrangements of objects: they are logical arrangements of the simple, indestructible and unchangeable meanings of names.

This terminology is notoriously complex but it is at least systematic and relatively precise. In order to help fix it in our minds, it may help to draw the following diagram:

PROPOSITIONS & NAMES		SENSE & MEANING
Ordinary propositions ——— ultimately analyzable into	represent / have as their senses	——➤ Possible states ultimately break down into
Elementary propositions —— consisting of	represent / have as their senses	——➤ States of affairs consisting of
Names ———————	designate / have as their meanings	——————➤ Objects

Looking at this, we can see that Wittgenstein suggests that it belongs to the concept of proposition that every proposition is ultimately analyzable into 'elementary propositions' made up of 'names' with simple, indestructible, and unchangeable meanings (or 'objects'). Furthermore, he suggests that anyone with a firm enough grasp of the concept of the proposition should – with a little help from the *Tractatus*! – come to see this connection. In this respect, it could be said that one of the main aims of the *Tractatus* is simply to clarify the concept of proposition: to clarify it so that the relation between ordinary and elementary propositions becomes clear – just as, when one clarifies the concept of bachelor, one comes to see the relation between being a bachelor and being a man, or between being a bachelor and being unmarried. Once again, for reasons we will consider later, the analogy with the concept of bachelor is problematic here. Here, I am merely using it to emphasize that, for Wittgenstein, anyone with a full understanding of the concept of proposition will see that ordinary, everyday language on the surface is ultimately analyzable in this way. They will see that, at the ultimate level of analysis, elementary propositions have states of affairs as their senses and that elementary propositions are made up of names with simple, indestructible and unchangeable meanings (or objects). In the next section, we will go on to consider why, precisely, Wittgenstein believes analyzability into elementary propositions to be part and parcel of the concept of proposition.

In Summary

–   According to Wittgenstein, all ordinary propositions in natural languages can ultimately be analyzed into 'elementary propositions'.
–   'Elementary propositions' are logical arrangements of 'names'. Each 'elementary proposition' represents a 'state of affairs': the 'state of affairs' represented by an 'elementary proposition' is the sense of that proposition. Each 'name' designates one and only one simple, indestructible, and unchangeable meaning – or 'object'.
–   'States of affairs' – the senses of 'elementary propositions' – are the most basic possible states, the more basic possibilities. States of affairs are logical arrangements of 'objects': they are logical arrangements of the simple, indestructible and unchangeable meanings of 'names'.

vii.   SIMPLE MEANINGS AND THE DETERMINACY OF SENSE

As we have seen, in the Tractarian order of things the ordinary propositions of everyday language are ultimately analyzable into 'elementary propositions' consisting of 'names', where each 'name' designates one and only one simple, unchangeable and indestructible meaning (or 'object'). In Wittgenstein's view, this is something that belongs to the very concept of proposition – as intrinsically as, for instance, it belongs to the concept of bachelor that bachelors should be unmarried. This raises a fairly obvious difficulty, however. For whereas the concept of bachelor is relatively straightforward and familiar to us (so that we can easily understand that bachelors must be unmarried), the concept of proposition in the sense Wittgenstein uses it is neither straightforward nor familiar. It is worth taking a moment, then, to explain why, according to Wittgenstein, it belongs to the concept of proposition that all propositions should be analyzable into 'elementary propositions' consisting of 'names'.

Wittgenstein's thinking on this issue can be outlined in the following way (don't worry – I will explain each step in a moment):

(A) It belongs to the concept of proposition that the sense of a proposition is determinate.
  AND
(B) If the senses of propositions are determinate, then propositions must be analyzable into 'elementary propositions' consisting of 'names' with simple, indestructible and unchangeable meanings.
  THEREFORE:
(C) It belongs to the concept of proposition that propositions must be analyzable into 'elementary propositions' consisting of 'names' with unchangeable, indestructible and simple meanings.

Examining these points, it is relatively easy to see why (C) might follow from (A) and (B), if we accept (A) and (B) in the first place. It is less easy to see why we should accept (A) and (B) at all! Let us therefore consider Wittgenstein's reasons for accepting (A) and (B) – and indeed what they mean in the context of the *Tractatus*.

Wittgenstein's reasons for accepting (A) and (B) in the *Tractatus* are both complex and problematic. Indeed, as we will see in later chapters, Wittgenstein himself would in later life come to reject his earlier thinking in this area. Nevertheless, it is important to give at least some idea of his reasons for endorsing (A) and (B) at this earlier stage in his philosophy – so let us consider each in turn.

The first question is, therefore: why does Wittgenstein endorse (A)? Why does he suggest that it belongs to the concept of proposition that the sense of a proposition must be determinate? In order to answer this question, it is useful to remember the distinction we drew earlier between a sentence and a proposition. A sentence can be used to represent a variety of possible states: it can be given a variety of senses. When a sentence is used to represent one particular possible state (one particular possibility) rather than another, it becomes a proposition. A proposition is a specific statement about a specific possible state – one that is expressed by means of a sentence. According to Wittgenstein, the sense of a proposition is something very precise: it is one fixed, clearly demarcated and differentiated possibility. Wittgenstein expresses this by saying that the sense of a proposition is determinate.

For Wittgenstein, the senses of all propositions are determinate – even those of ordinary propositions in natural languages. This may come as something of a surprise. After all, we have just been discussing the fact that, in his view, language is very imprecise at the non-analyzed level. Why then does he suddenly suggest that even ordinary propositions in natural languages have precisely demarcated senses? The answer to this question lies once more in the distinction between a sentence and a proposition. For Wittgenstein, ordinary propositions appear ambiguous because they are expressed by means of ambiguous sentences and words – the sentences and words of natural languages. Nevertheless, for all of their apparent ambiguity, ordinary propositions – if they really are propositions – have precise and clearly demarcated senses. Let us illustrate this by means of an example. Imagine that we are discussing what programme is being shown on the television. And imagine that, as part of this discussion, I put to you the proposition: 'The bald eagle expert is on the television'. In other words, imagine that I use the sentence 'The bald eagle expert is on the television' to make a particular statement about a particular possible state – that I use this sentence to express a genuine proposition. Since my proposition is expressed by means of an ambiguous sentence, it may be that you will find it confusing and ask for a clarification. One way in which I could clarify the sense of my proposition would be by giving you the beginnings of its logical analysis. For instance, I might say 'the eagle expert who is bald is on the television' (or, if I am the fastidious, logically inclined type of friend: 'the eagle expert is bald and the eagle expert is on the television'). This rudimentary first step in the logical analysis of the proposition would make it clear to you that my statement concerns an expert in eagles who happens to be bald – rather than, for example, an expert in bald eagles (perhaps one with a perfect coiffure!). Logical analysis clarifies the sense of a proposition and also shows that its sense is quite precise. If I genuinely use the sentence 'The bald eagle expert is on television' to express a proposition, then it should be possible to pinpoint the determinate sense of this proposition by means of logical analysis.

Still, natural languages are notoriously ambiguous and their ambiguity can be the source of much confusion. We can easily become confused as to whether a sentence expresses one proposition or another (whether it is used to represent one possible state or another, quite different one). If a sentence really is being used to express a proposition, however, then the proposition in question will have a determinate sense, according to Wittgenstein – whether we have interpreted the sentence correctly or not at first glance. If the proposition is a proposition at all, it will represent one particular, precisely delineated possibility: a possibility that can be identified with exactitude, whose boundaries, as it were, are perfectly demarcated; a possibility that is, therefore, clearly distinct from all others and which we can in all likelihood start to identify by means of a few clarifying questions (i.e. by beginning the process of logical analysis).

For Wittgenstein, in the *Tractatus*, this is simply part and parcel of the concept of proposition. After all, in the *Tractatus*, a proposition is a sentence that is used to represent one particular possible state. If possible states were not precisely demarcated, if they did not have fixed, clearly drawn boundaries, then they would run the risk of becoming indistinguishable from each other. But then the very notion of a proposition representing one particular possible state – rather than another – would be at risk. Let us consider another example to illustrate this point. Imagine that we are discussing our neighbours, who are animal-crazy and have all sorts of creatures living in their house. And imagine that, as part of that discussion, I say 'I just met Toto: Toto is a chicken', to which you reply by shaking your head and saying 'Toto is a kitten'. Consider the two propositions 'Toto is a chicken' and 'Toto is a kitten'. 'Toto is a chicken' represents one particular possible state: it represents a possible state that involves being a chicken. 'Toto is a kitten', in turn, represents a different possible state, one that involves being a kitten. If there were no clearly demarcated differences between being a chicken and being a kitten, the two possible states represented by these propositions would blur into each other. Wittgenstein's worry seems to have been that, if possible states were not rigourously identifiable and distinct from each other, if they did not have precisely delineated boundaries, the very idea of a proposition representing one particular possible state – rather than another – would be lost. That is, for propositions to represent particular possible states (ones that are clearly distinct from one another), possible states must have fixed, precisely delineated boundaries – in this example, this involves there being a clearly demarcated difference between the possibility of being a chicken and that of being a kitten. Possible states must have precise identities that make them clearly distinct from each other. There can be no grey areas when it comes to possible states.

This, then, is why Wittgenstein endorses (A); in his view, it is part and parcel of the concept of proposition that the sense of a proposition is determinate – a proposition represents a fixed, sharply delineated possible state, one that can (at least in principle!) be identified with precision and that is, therefore, clearly distinct from others. All propositions have determinate senses in his view, even those expressed by sentences in natural languages. But in addition, Wittgenstein suggests that, for the sense of a proposition to be determinate, this proposition must ultimately be analyzable into 'elementary propositions' consisting of 'names' with unchangeable, indestructible and simple meanings. Why does he suggest this? In other words, why does Wittgenstein also endorse (B)?

Well, this is a very complex issue, one that has led to major scholarly disagreements. In fact, there is no doubt that the *Tractatus*' discussion of this question is highly unsatisfactory in many respects, and Wittgenstein himself later comes to reject it. Nevertheless, it is worth giving an idea of his position on this question in the *Tractatus* if only so we can see why he later retreats from it. What, therefore, is the relation, in the *Tractatus*, between sense being determinate and propositions being analyzable into 'elementary propositions' made up of 'names' with unchangeable, indestructible and simple meanings? Or, to put it differently: why must 'objects' (the meanings of 'names') be unchangeable, indestructible and simple if sense is to be determinate?

If the senses of ordinary propositions are to be determinate, ordinary propositions must represent specific, precisely identifiable and distinct possible states: in other words, the possible states that are the senses of ordinary propositions must have perfectly delineated boundaries. According to Wittgenstein, possible states are ultimately made up of states of affairs, which are the senses of 'elementary propositions'. If states of affairs did not themselves have perfectly delineated boundaries, neither would the more complex possible states that they produce and the result would be that sense in general would not be determinate. It is clear, therefore, that, for sense to be determinate, states of affairs must be specific, precisely identifiable and distinct possibilities: states of affairs must have sharp boundaries. In Wittgenstein's view, however, states of affairs would not be specific in the required way if the objects that made them up could change or be destroyed. The question we are considering at the moment is: why does Wittgenstein believe that, for states of affairs to be specific possibilities, objects must be unchangeable and indestructible? And how does this relate to the idea that objects must be simple?

Wittgenstein's thinking on this issue seems to have run along the following lines. If the objects that make up states of affairs were all constantly changing or being destroyed, there would be nothing to guarantee the specificity of states of affairs: in other words, there would be nothing to guarantee that states of affairs were specific, precisely identifiable and distinct possibilities. This is rather a complex idea. Let us consider an example to illustrate it – an example which, although problematic in many respects, helps, I think, to throw light on this point. Imagine a house built from bricks. If the bricks that made up this house were constantly changing (e.g. if they were constantly changing shape, colour, material, location in space, etc.), it would become impossible to regard the resulting structure as one particular or specific house – as one house clearly identifiable and distinct from all other houses. After all, the resulting structure would itself be constantly changing shape, colours, materials, and it would spread over different areas of space, etc. In fact, even if the bricks never happened to change, so long as they were capable of changing, there would be nothing to guarantee the specificity of the house: there would be nothing to guarantee that the house would always remain one particular, precisely identifiable structure, one clearly distinct from all others, etc.

The relationship between states of affairs (the senses of 'elementary propositions') and objects (the meanings of 'names') is, in some respects, similar to the relationship between this house and the bricks that make it up. Without unchangeable and indestructible 'objects', there would be nothing to guarantee the specificity of states of affairs: there would be nothing to guarantee states of affairs understood as possibilities with fixed boundaries, possibilities that could be identified with precision and that were clearly distinct from each other. In that case, however, there would be nothing to guarantee the specificity of the possible states produced by combining states of affairs. In other words, without unchangeable and indestructible meanings (without 'objects'), sense would not, at any level, be determinate. So, for sense to be determinate, for propositions to represent specific possible states, objects must be unchangeable and indestructible.

Why must objects also be simple, however? We touched upon this idea earlier on. Wittgenstein believes that, for objects to be unchangeable and indestructible in the required way, they also need to be simple. A complex object can change or be destroyed in that its components can be reorganized, replaced with others or altogether pulled apart. Simple objects – simple meanings – are not vulnerable in this way: being simple, they do not have components that could be reorganized, replaced or pulled apart. As a result, they are guaranteed to be unchangeable and indestructible and this, in turn, guarantees the determinacy of sense.

All of this means that, without simple, indestructible and unchangeable objects at the basic level of linguistic structure, 'elementary propositions' and the more complex ordinary propositions that they produce would not have determinate senses. And if that were the case, they would not be propositions at all: for it is part and parcel of the concept of proposition that propositions have determinate senses. This, in a nutshell, is the heart Wittgenstein's position on the relation between simplicity of meaning and determinacy of sense.

So we have seen, then, that for Wittgenstein, it belongs to the very concept of proposition that sense should be determinate. He also suggests that, if sense is to be determinate, propositions must ultimately be analyzable into 'elementary propositions' consisting of 'names' with simple, indestructible and unchangeable meanings. This enables him to conclude that it belongs to the very concept of proposition that propositions should ultimately be analyzable in this way. And that is why, as we saw at the start of this section, Wittgenstein accepts (A) and (B) and, as a result, he also accepts (C). Wittgenstein summarizes this idea with beautiful concision in the following entry:

The requirement that simple signs be possible is the requirement that sense be determinate. (TLP 3.23)

In Summary

- It is part and parcel of the concept of proposition that the sense of a proposition is determinate. A proposition is a sentence that is used to represent one specific possible state, a possible state that is clearly distinct from others. Propositions therefore have fixed, clearly demarcated possible states as their senses.
- If possible states were not ultimately made up of 'states of affairs' consisting of simple, indestructible and unchangeable meanings (or 'objects'), the determinacy of sense would not be guaranteed. Possible states would be at risk of blurring into each other; there would be no guarantee that they would retain their fixed, clearly demarcated boundaries.
- It therefore belongs to the concept of proposition that propositions are analyzable into 'elementary propositions' consisting of 'names' with simple, indestructible and unchangeable meanings (or 'objects').

viii. SENSE AND MEANING

At this stage, it is worth taking a moment to elaborate a little more fully on a distinction that is crucial to Wittgenstein: the distinction between sense and meaning. According to Wittgenstein, only propositions have sense; and only names – i.e. the names that emerge at the ultimate level of analysis, the names that make up elementary propositions – have meaning. The two are mutually exclusive: propositions have sense, but do not have meaning; names have meaning, but do not have sense. The reason for this is that the notion of meaning and that of sense are very different in his view.

One way of making the difference clearer is to consider the distinction between what a proposition is about and what a proposition represents. This distinction is useful in that, although it does not map perfectly on to the distinction between meaning and sense, it is a close parallel to it. In order to clarify the contrast between what a proposition is about and what it represents, we are, once again, going to look at examples that are not ideal (in that they do not fit Wittgenstein's intentions perfectly), but which do serve to throw light on these notions. Having looked at these examples, we will go on to see why they are less than ideal and also why they are, nevertheless, the only examples available to us.

The question before us is, therefore: what is the distinction between what a proposition is about and what it represents? Let us take as examples two propositions we introduced earlier (in the context of the astronomy lesson): the propositions 'The earth revolves around the sun' and 'The sun revolves around the earth'. What, we may ask, are these propositions about? One answer that might come naturally to us (especially if we are unfamiliar with Wittgenstein) is that both of these propositions are about the planet earth and our nearest star, the sun: the two propositions are therefore about the same things. It is clear, however, that these two propositions do not represent the same possibility – these do not represent the same possible way in which reality might be. This becomes clear when one considers that these two propositions differ with respect to their truth and falsity: 'The earth revolves around the sun' is true, it represents a possibility that obtains in reality; 'The sun revolves around the earth', in contrast, is false – it still represents a possibility, but one that does not obtain in reality. Although we might regard these two propositions as being about the same things, they clearly represent different possibilities. This shows that there is an important difference between what a proposition is about and what a proposition represents.

In order to further clarify the difference between the two, imagine a scientist attempting to give a description of the universe in which we live. In order to describe the universe, it is not enough for the scientist to simply list what things there are in the universe. It is not enough to come up with a list of the contents of this universe, a list of the type: 'earth, sun, moon', etc. For such a list of contents applies to a variety of other possible universes as well: universes in which the sun revolves around the earth; ones in which the earth revolves around the moon, etc. Merely giving a list of contents does not help to pinpoint our universe, as opposed to all those other possible ones. In order to describe our universe, we need to do more than just give a list of contents: we need full propositions that describe how the things that our universe contains (the sun, the earth, the moon, etc.) are organized. This description involves representing certain possibilities rather than others; it involves advancing propositions that affirm certain possible states rather than others. A true description of our universe would include the proposition 'The earth revolves around the sun', but not the proposition 'The sun revolves around the earth' – even though these propositions appear to be about the same things.

For Wittgenstein, the distinction between what a proposition is about and what it represents is absolutely fundamental. It is partly for this reason that he begins the *Tractatus* by noting:

The world is all that is the case. (TLP 1)

The world is the totality of facts, not of things. (TLP 1.1)

If, like our scientist, we were trying to give a description of the world (and a true one at that!), it would not be enough for us to provide a mere list of things – a list of the contents of this world. Instead, we would need to present a series of true propositions, of propositions representing those possible states that obtain in reality as facts. Providing a true description involves advancing propositions that represent possible states that obtain as facts; it does not involve merely presenting lists of what these propositions are about.

For Wittgenstein, the distinction between what a proposition is about and what it represents is important because it closely parallels the distinction between meaning and sense. In his view, what a proposition is about relates to the notion of meaning; in contrast, what a proposition represents relates to the notion of sense. The sense of a proposition is what a proposition represents: it is the possible state – the possibility – represented by the proposition. Capturing what the proposition is about, in contrast, involves capturing meaning.

The reason why Wittgenstein would be unhappy with the above examples is that, in his view, ordinary propositions are not about what they appear to be. In his view, it is misleading to claim that 'The earth revolves around the sun' and 'The sun revolves around the earth' are about the planet earth and the sun. For this could be taken to suggest that the word 'earth' has a meaning – its meaning being the planet earth, that complex object floating in space on which we live; and that the word 'sun' has another meaning – its meaning being the star which is nearest to us, that other complex object floating in space. That is, these examples might be taken to suggest that ordinary words have as their meanings things that can change and be destroyed – large, complex things such as planets and stars. According to Wittgenstein, this view would be entirely mistaken, however. For meanings are the ultimate building blocks of sense. Meanings (the meanings of names) must be simple, unchangeable and indestructible, if sense is to be determinate. And sense, as we saw above, has to be determinate, if it is to be sense at all, for the earlier Wittgenstein.

If we follow this through to its ultimate conclusion, then ordinary propositions are not about what they appear, on the surface, to be. They are not about the kind of complex, changeable and destructible things we come across in reality. Instead, propositions are about the simple, indestructible and unchangeable meanings that emerge only at the final stage of logical analysis: propositions are about the simple, indestructible and unchangeable 'objects' that are the meanings of 'names'. It is a mistake, therefore, to say that the word 'earth' has the planet earth as its meaning. Instead, we should concentrate on the idea that the propositions expressed by means of such words (propositions such as 'The earth revolves around the sun') can in principle be analyzed all the way to the level of 'elementary propositions', where 'names' with genuine meanings finally emerge. Given all this, it is clearly far from ideal to be using propositions such as 'The earth revolves around the sun', as I have, to illustrate the distinction between what propositions are about and what they represent. Since we have no examples of 'elementary propositions' or of 'names', however, the only way to convey, albeit imperfectly, this distinction is to do so by means of such ordinary propositions. This is just a glimpse of the problems that we, and Wittgenstein himself, have when we try to talk about the perfectly ordered, entirely logical substructure that the *Tractatus* posits while using our ordinary language to do it!

As we have just seen, meaning, for Wittgenstein, is essentially simple. Sense, by contrast, is essentially complex. The most basic senses are 'states of affairs': they are the senses of the most basic of propositions, the senses of the 'elementary propositions'. Even these most basic of senses are complex structures, though: after all, as we saw in Section 6, a 'state of affairs' is an arrangement of several 'objects', of several simple meanings.

In Summary

- Sense relates to the notion of what a proposition represents; meaning relates to the notion of what a proposition is about.
- Only propositions have senses (that is, only propositions represent). Only names (i.e. only the names found at the ultimate

level of analysis, those that make up elementary propositions) have meanings. Meaning is essentially simple; sense is essentially complex.

– Ordinary propositions are not about what they appear to be. The ordinary words of ordinary propositions do not have meanings; rather ordinary propositions are ultimately analyzable into elementary propositions consisting of names that do have meanings. In a way, therefore, all propositions are really about the simple meanings of names.

ix. LOGICAL ANALYSIS AND TRUTH-TABLES

Before we draw this chapter to a close, I would like to discuss one of the most innovative aspects of the *Tractatus*: the notion of a truth-table. As we saw earlier, for Wittgenstein, the idea that propositions have sense is intimately connected to the idea that they are determinately either true or false. In the previous section, when we were discussing the propositions 'The earth revolves around the sun' and 'The sun revolves around the earth', we saw that one of the ways to show that these propositions have different senses (in spite of their being apparently about the same things) is to show that they have different truth-values.

Having a sense and having a truth-value go hand in hand, according to Wittgenstein. This is not surprising, since, in his view, a proposition has a sense if it represents a possible state; and for a state to be possible is for it to determinately either obtain or fail to obtain. But this, in turn, is precisely what gives propositions their determinate truth-values; for a proposition is true when the possible state it represents obtains (when it is realized as a fact in reality) and it is false when the possible state it represents does not obtain. This goes to show that for a proposition to have sense is for it to have a truth-value, in Wittgenstein's view.

Let us look at this issue a little more closely. As we saw earlier, the ordinary propositions of natural languages can be logically analyzed: they can be broken down into more basic propositions, which, in turn, can themselves be broken down into even more basic propositions, and so on – a process that continues until one reaches the most basic of propositions: elementary proposition consisting of names with simple, indestructible and unchangeable meanings. In Wittgenstein's view, ordinary propositions can be analyzed into more basic propositions because they result from applying 'logical operations' (as they are called in philosophy) to these more basic propositions. Let us use an example to illustrate this point. Consider again the proposition 'Ivan is a bachelor'. This proposition can be logically analyzed into two more basic propositions: 'Ivan is a man' and 'Ivan is unmarried'. Another way of looking at this is to say that 'Ivan is a bachelor' is the product of applying the logical operation 'AND' to two more basic propositions: 'Ivan is a man'; 'Ivan is unmarried'. The idea here is that logical operations on propositions produce other propositions, just as mathematical operations on numbers produce other numbers. So, for instance, the logical operation: 'Ivan is a man' AND 'Ivan is unmarried' produces another proposition, namely 'Ivan is a bachelor' – similarly, in mathematics, the operation 2 + 3 produces another number, namely 5.

According to Wittgenstein, there are two basic logical operations: conjunction ('AND') and negation ('NOT'). Propositions result from successively applying these two operations to other, more basic propositions. Note for instance that, in the above example, 'Ivan is unmarried' is equivalent to: NOT-'Ivan is married'. We can now see, therefore, that 'Ivan is a bachelor' is the result of the combined logical operation: 'Ivan is a man' AND NOT-'Ivan is married'. Or, to put it differently: 'Ivan is a bachelor' results from the conjunction of 'Ivan is a man' and the negation of 'Ivan is married'.

Ordinary propositions result from applying logical operations to more basic propositions. Since ordinary propositions are ultimately analyzable into elementary propositions, it is clear that ordinary propositions ultimately result from applying a complicated series of logical operations to these elementary propositions. If we had the complete analysis of some proposition (if we had its analysis to the level of elementary propositions), we would be able to see that this proposition results from applying a very complex series of logical operations to 'elementary propositions'. As we saw earlier, however, we have no instances of the complete analysis of any proposition. We can therefore only illustrate how logical operations work by using examples that involve ordinary, non-elementary propositions, such as 'Ivan is a bachelor', 'Ivan is a man', 'Ivan is married', etc.

Wittgenstein did not invent the notion of a logical operation, but he did push forward our understanding of it. There was one particular aspect of the way in which logical operations had been portrayed by philosophers before him that especially concerned him.

Wittgenstein was concerned that the traditional philosophical way of presenting logical operations led to serious confusions as to the nature of these operations. Consider, once again, the proposition 'Ivan is a bachelor'. This proposition results from the conjunction of 'Ivan is a man' and 'Ivan is unmarried'. Traditionally, the logical operation of conjunction would have been represented by a sign – for instance the sign '&'. 'Ivan is a bachelor' would therefore have been presented as equivalent to p & q, where p is 'Ivan is a man' and q is 'Ivan is unmarried'. One of the problems with this way of presenting logical operations is that it gives very much the impression that the sign for the operation (here, '&') is on a par with the signs for the propositions (p, q): it gives the impression '&', p and q are the same kinds of signs. This, in turn, creates the impression that logical operations are in some important respects analogous to propositions with senses: that '&' might, like p, have some special logical sense (or, perhaps, some special logical meaning). In Wittgenstein's view, this would be deeply misleading. Logical operations are entirely unlike propositions (or names): they are (logical) processes that propositions are put through, and not as it were things in their own right.

This and other considerations led Wittgenstein to pioneer a new way of presenting logical operations: the truth-table. Truth-tables have, for Wittgenstein, the significant advantage of presenting logical operations without the need for signs for these operations, signs such as '&'. In this way, truth-tables avoid the danger of creating the impression that logical operations and propositions are analogous in kind: in fact, truth-tables show (they manifest, they make clear) that logical operations are totally unlike propositions with senses. Consider, for instance, the following truth-table:

	p	q	r
1	T	T	T
2	T	F	F
3	F	T	F
4	F	F	F

This is the truth-table for conjunction (for the logical operation AND). Here, r is the proposition that results from applying the logical operation of conjunction (AND) to the propositions p and q: r is p & q. This truth-table shows what happens to the truth-value of r (p & q) when the truth-values of p and q change. In other words, it shows how the truth-values of p and q affect the truth-value of the conjunction p & q (or r).

Truth-tables are relatively easy to read. Each line of Ts and Fs presents one possible combination of truth-values: T indicates that the proposition under consideration is true, F indicates that it is false. For example, in the above truth-table, line 1 shows that, if p is true and q is true, then the resulting r (p&q) is true as well. Line 2 shows that, if p is true and q false, then the resulting r is false. Line 3 shows that, if p is false and q is true, then the resulting r is false. Finally, line 4 shows that, if p is false and q is false, then the resulting r is false. Imagine, for instance, that p stands for 'Ivan is a man', q stands for 'Ivan is unmarried', and r stands 'Ivan is a bachelor' (i.e. for: 'Ivan is a man'& 'Ivan is unmarried'). In that case, line 1 can be taken to show that, if 'Ivan is a man' and 'Ivan is unmarried' are both true, then 'Ivan is a bachelor' is also as a whole true. Line 2, in turn, shows that, if 'Ivan is a man' is true and 'Ivan is unmarried' is false, 'Ivan is a bachelor' as a whole is false – and so on down the table.

The truth-table for negation is the simplest truth-table there is. Let us say that n is the negation of p: in other words, let us say that n is NOT-p (or, as it is more traditionally represented, ~p or ¬p). If p is true, its negation n will be false; if p is false, its negation n will be true. For instance, if 'Ivan is a man' is true, its negation (NOT-'Ivan is a man' or 'Ivan is not a man') is false; if 'Ivan is a man' is false, its negation ('Ivan is not a man') is true. The truth-table of negation is therefore simply as follows:

p	n
T	F
F	T

For Wittgenstein, conjunction (AND) and negation (NOT) are the most basic logical operations: they are, in fact, the foundations of all other logical operations. Consider for instance the logical operation NEITHER: neither-p nor-q. Although, at first glance, it may look like this operation has nothing to do with those of conjunction and negation, it is in fact very simply built up from them: indeed, neither-p nor-q is equivalent to NOT-p AND NOT-q (also written as ¬p&¬q). Let us illustrated this by means of an example. Take the following two propositions: 'Rosa will be flying to Paris' (let us call this p); 'Rosa will be flying to Madrid' (let us call this q). If Rosa will be flying to neither of these two cities, we may want to express this as follows: neither 'Rosa will be flying to Paris' nor 'Rosa will be flying to Madrid'. But, from the point of view of logic, this is just the same as: NOT-'Rosa will be flying to Paris' AND NOT-'Rosa will be flying to Madrid'. In other words, 'neither-p nor-q' is logically equivalent to 'NOT-p AND NOT-q'. Conjunction and negation are the foundations of the logical operation 'neither-p nor-q': 'neither-p nor-q' is produced by combining conjunction and negation in a particular way, and this is shown in that it can be expressed in terms of conjunction and negation alone.

Since 'neither-p nor-q' results from combining conjunction and negation in a particular way, it is not surprising that its truth-table can be built on the basis of the truth-tables for conjunction and negation. The truth-table for 'neither-p nor-q' is as follows:

	p	q	¬p	¬q	¬p&¬q (neither-p nor-q)
1	T	T	F	F	F
2	T	F	F	T	F
3	F	T	T	F	F
4	F	F	T	T	T

This truth-table shows that neither-p nor-q is equivalent to NOT-p AND NOT-q (or ¬p&¬q). Take a look at the first line of the truth-table. This first line shows that: if p is true, then ¬p (that is, NOT-p) is false; if q is true, then ¬q is false; in that case, ¬p&¬q as a whole is false. This can also be read as follows: if p is true and q is true, then neither-p nor-q as a whole is false. If it is true that 'Rosa will be flying to Paris' and it is also true that 'Rosa will be flying to Madrid', then it is false that: neither 'Rosa will be flying to Paris' nor 'Rosa will be flying to Madrid'. From the point of view of logic, the operation NEITHER (neither-p nor-q) is the same as the operation NOT-p AND NOT-q (¬p&¬q): the operation NEITHER (neither-p nor-q) yields the same results in terms of truth-value dependence as the operation NOT-p AND NOT-q.

In fact, Wittgenstein suggests that all logical operations ultimately come down to particular combinations of the operations of negation

and conjunction. They can all therefore be presented by constructing
truth-tables based on those of negation and conjunction, as we just
did for neither-p nor-q. Furthermore, truth-tables mean that we no
longer need to use signs for the logical operations themselves (signs
such as '&', '¬,' 'neither', etc.) in order to clarify which logical
operation is being presented. Indeed, an experienced logician would
quickly be able to work out, merely by looking at the truth-value
combinations in a truth-table, which logical operation is at work in
each case. So, a logician looking at the following truth-table:

p	q	r
T	T	T
T	F	F
F	T	F
F	F	F

would quickly be able to work out, by considering how the Ts and
the Fs are arranged, that this must be the truth-table for conjunction.
Similarly, he or she would be able to work out that the following is a
truth-table for negation:

p	r
T	F
F	T

and that the following is a truth-table for NOT-p AND NOT-q (or,
which is the same, for neither-p nor-q):

p	q	r
T	T	F
T	F	F
F	T	F
F	F	T

A competent logician would be able to work this out, merely by
studying the various combinations of truth-values appearing in
each truth-table – even if no signs for any logical operations (such as
'&', '¬', etc.) appeared in the truth-table. That is, they would be

able to work this out even if there was nothing to indicate that: in the first truth-table, r stands for p&q; in the second r stands for ¬p; and in the third r stands for ¬p&¬q. The signs for logical operations are shown to be redundant by truth-tables, whereas the signs for propositions are not. According to Wittgenstein, this shows that the signs for logical operations are not on a par with the signs that are used to express propositions (indeed, with 'names'). Logical operations are processes that propositions can be put through, but they are altogether unlike propositions (or 'names'). Logical operations are not analogous to propositions: they do not represent, they do not have special, logical senses. And they are not analogous to 'names' either: they do not have special logical meanings.

In Summary

–   Ordinary propositions result from applying logical operations to more basic propositions. Ultimately, all propositions result from applying logical operations to the elementary propositions that make them up.
–   Truth-tables show that the truth-value of a proposition results from logically combining the truth-values of the more basic propositions that make it up. Ultimately, the truth-values of all propositions are dependent on those of the elementary propositions that make them up.
–   Conjunction (AND) and negation (NOT) are the most basic logical operations and the foundations of all other logical operations. All logical operations (e.g. neither-p nor-q) can be presented in terms of conjunction and negation alone. This can be shown by means of truth-tables.
–   Truth-tables enable logicians to do away with the signs for logical operations (signs such as '&' and '¬'). In Wittgenstein's view, the use of these signs is misleading: writing p&q, for instance, gives the mistaken impression that '&' – the sign for conjunction – is analogous to the signs for the propositions, here p and q. This in turn creates the misleading impression that logical operations represent or have senses (perhaps special, logical senses). This, according to Wittgenstein, is fundamentally incorrect: logical operations are not analogous to propositions – they are processes that propositions are put through.

x. CONCLUSION

In this chapter we have covered a great deal of ground and tackled some notoriously thorny problems – some of which continue to divide philosophers to this day! That said, we are leaving open several important questions, particularly concerning Wittgenstein's earlier understanding of propositions. Some of these we will be considering in the next chapter; others we will only be examining in the conclusion to Part I. Some of the notions we have merely hinted at in this chapter – notions such as those of use, of process, and the idea of someone exercising an ability in a particular area of expertise – will come to the fore at that point.

Before we are able to turn to such matters, however, we must first consider the relation that exists for Wittgenstein between thoughts and propositions, and the way in which – in his view – thoughts and propositions are essentially pictorial. That is what we will turn to in the next chapter.

CHAPTER 2

THOUGHTS AND THE SELF

i. INTRODUCTION: PHILOSOPHY – NOT PSYCHOLOGY

The *Tractatus* contains a series of very interesting discussions concerning thought, the mind and the self. This might seem surprising. What exactly – we may ask – is a philosophical book doing by discussing these notions? Isn't this more appropriately the purview of a different discipline, such as that of psychology? What can a philosopher tell us about thought, the mind and the self that would not be better explained by a psychology specialist? Wittgenstein suggests that this reaction is mistaken. There is, in his view, a distinctive philosophical approach to questions about thought, the mind and the self: one that is altogether different from the psychological approach and which, in some ways, is more fundamental.

According to Wittgenstein, psychology aims to uncover the *facts* about thought, the mind and the self. In particular, it aims to uncover the mental, neurological and environmental mechanisms that give rise – *in reality* – to certain thought processes and to one's sense of self. Wittgenstein tells us that psychology is one of the natural sciences; as such, it is primarily interested in providing true descriptions of the facts, as they obtain in reality, and to do so by means of empirical investigations. The philosophical approach to thought, the mind and the self is very different. The aim of philosophy is not to establish facts, but to clarify the concepts we use. This task of conceptual clarification may appear menial, when compared to the scientific task of uncovering and accurately portraying facts. For Wittgenstein, however, it is emphatically not so. Indeed, he sees the philosophical task of clarifying concepts as in some respects more fundamental than the task of uncovering and describing facts.

In order to explain this, let us consider again an example that Wittgenstein himself does not use, but which is helpful for illustrative purposes. Consider again the notion of a bachelor. There are at least two possible approaches we can take when dealing with this notion. The first one involves trying to provide an accurate description of the facts about bachelors: how many there are in reality, what their ages and occupations are, what they look like and what clothes they wear, etc. The second approach aims to throw light on the concept itself: for instance, by clarifying that the concept of a bachelor is that of an unmarried man, rather than an unmarried woman. One of the reasons why this task of conceptual clarification can be regarded as more fundamental is that, in order to uncover the facts about bachelors (how many there are, etc.), one needs to be clear as to what one is looking for: before I can go out on a bachelor-counting expedition, I need to have a clear grasp of what I mean by the term in the first place. It is important to have a clear grasp of a concept – and therefore, if necessary, to clarify it – before one attempts to establish the *facts* relating to this concept: in this respect, the philosophical task of conceptual clarification is more fundamental than that of establishing the facts.

For Wittgenstein, philosophy has something interesting to say about thought, the mind and the self because the philosophical approach to these notions is altogether distinct from – and in some ways more fundamental than – the psychological approach. Psychology aims at establishing the facts concerning thought, the mind and the self; philosophy aims at clarifying the concepts themselves, a task which is to a degree prior to that of investigating the facts.

Philosophy is not one of the natural sciences. (TLP 4.111)

Philosophy aims at the logical clarification of thoughts. [. . . It results in] the clarification of propositions. (TLP 4.112)

Psychology is no more closely related to philosophy than any other natural science. (TLP 4.1121)

This might make it sound as if Wittgenstein thinks that psychologists have been mishandling concepts such as those of thought, the mind and the self or using the language in which these concepts are expressed in an incorrect or arbitrary manner. It might make it sound as if philosophers are needed in order to sort out the conceptual mess created by psychologists – perhaps even as if psychologists and other natural scientists need to study the *Tractatus* before they can proceed with their business of uncovering the facts about the world. In reality – thankfully, perhaps – nothing could be further from the truth. In Wittgenstein's view, the way in which language is used in psychology is perfectly in order. He does think that concepts such as those of thought, the mind and the self have been mishandled in the past, but not by psychologists: these concepts have been mishandled by *philosophers*, notably among them by his friend and mentor Bertrand Russell. In Wittgenstein's view, Russell and other philosophers before him failed to realize that the philosophical and the psychological approaches to thought, the mind and the self are – and need to be kept – altogether separate. As we will see later in this chapter, Wittgenstein believes that these philosophers mistakenly attempted to fuse together the conceptual approach which is the legitimate purview of philosophy with the factual approach of psychology – and *that* certainly resulted in a conceptual mess. Instead of throwing light on the concepts, these philosophers created a psycho-philosophical hybrid approach that is profoundly problematic – an approach that is at the root of some of the most entrenched and apparently unresolvable problems in traditional philosophy.

Wittgenstein thinks that this confusion – and the problems that come with it – can be entirely stripped away if we adopt a proper, purely conceptual philosophical approach. In fact, he believes that many of these apparently unsolvable problems of philosophy can be revealed *not to be problems at all*. By sticking to the genuine task of philosophy – that of conceptual clarification – we can demonstrate that some of the most apparently intractable problems of philosophy simply vanish into thin air. Problems about which philosophers have been arguing for centuries disintegrate the moment that the underlying concepts have been sufficiently clarified. Wittgenstein's view is that this exciting, rather iconoclastic new approach threatens the very foundations of some of the traditional philosophical questions about being, reality and our world.

The philosophical task of conceptual clarification is more fundamental than that of establishing the facts, in that one cannot establish the facts that relate to a concept if one is confused about the concept in the first place. Psychologists and other natural scientists are not, however, confused about the concepts they employ. For Wittgenstein, conceptual confusion is a product of philosophy, not of the natural sciences. It is philosophers – not natural scientists – who need the intensive process of conceptual clarification that the *Tractatus* provides. Admittedly, Wittgenstein's intention is that philosophers should, through the *Tractatus*, achieve a degree of conceptual clarity that is far higher than is typical of scientific discourse. But that is because philosophers *need* this higher level of clarity: they need it because their conceptual confusions are so deep and so entrenched that only such a radical treatment can possibly remove them. (Wittgenstein thinks that natural scientists do not generate conceptual confusions in this way. They do not need to push their grasp of concepts as far as philosophers do, because their grasp of concepts is not confused in the first place – it is perfectly suited to their purposes. He thinks natural scientists are already as clear about their concepts as is required for the purpose of carrying out empirical investigations into the facts.)

For Wittgenstein, then, the process of intensive conceptual clarification that the *Tractatus* engages us in is extremely important. It is important, first of all, because the propensity towards conceptual confusion among philosophers is wide-ranging, deeply rooted and very damaging. And it is also important for another, perhaps more significant reason: for, as we will see in Chapter 3, this process of conceptual clarification has a fundamental ethical dimension.

In this chapter, we will consider Wittgenstein's approach to thought, the mind and the self in the *Tractatus*. We will begin by examining his views on the relation between thoughts and propositions and his suggestion that both are essentially pictorial. We will then be in a position to consider one of the most intriguing discussions of the *Tractatus*: the discussion of solipsism. As we will see, solipsism is one of those thoroughly entrenched traditional problems of philosophy which have been exercising philosophers for centuries, and which Wittgenstein believes is based on conceptually confused foundations that can be stripped entirely away.

This chapter will be organized as follows. In Section ii, we will consider Wittgenstein's suggestion that thoughts and propositions are essentially pictures; in Section iii, we will look at his discussion of the mind and the self; and in Section iv, we will introduce the philosophical problem of solipsism and examine Wittgenstein's treatment of it.

In Summary

- Psychology, like other natural sciences, aims at providing us with correct (i.e. true) descriptions of the facts. It does so by carrying out empirical investigations of the facts.
- Philosophy does not aim to provide true descriptions of the facts. Instead it aims to clarify concepts, to clarify what we mean by things. Such conceptual clarifications are fundamental in at least one important respect: if I am confused about my concepts, I will not be able to establish the facts that relate to them.
- For Wittgenstein, natural scientists are clear enough about the concepts they employ: they are as clear as is necessary for their purpose of carrying out empirical investigations of the facts. It is philosophers, not natural scientists, who require the intensive process of conceptual clarification that the *Tractatus* offers. The level of conceptual confusion in philosophy is so deep and so entrenched that it needs special, radical treatment.

ii. THOUGHTS AND PROPOSITIONS AS PICTURES

Wittgenstein's discussion of thought in the *Tractatus* aims to clarify the concept of a thought – more specifically, to clarify what is *essential* to this concept. The distinction between what is essential to a concept and what is merely accidental to it is one we discussed in Chapter 1. Consider again the concept of bachelor. In Chapter 1 we saw that, whereas being a man (rather than a woman) is an essential feature of this concept, being blond is not. Similarly, Wittgenstein's exploration of the concept of thought aims to clarify what is *essential* to this concept. According to Wittgenstein, when one considers what is essential to the concept of thought, one realizes that the concept is similar to that of a proposition. Although there are, of course, differences between the two concepts, there are also some very important similarities between them. As we saw in Chapter 1, a proposition is in essence an arrangement of signs (of words) that is used to represent one particular possible state. Wittgenstein's view is that a thought too is an arrangement of signs that represents a particular possible state. We will see that this is a crucial point of similarity between propositions and thoughts, for Wittgenstein. At the same time, there are also important differences between the concept of proposition and that of thought. One of the differences is that the signs that make up propositions – the words – are perceptible by the senses: the words written on this page can be perceived through the sense of sight, spoken words through the sense of hearing, words in Braille through the sense of touch, etc. The signs that make up thoughts, in contrast, are not perceivable through the senses: they are mental signs that have their existence within our minds, rather than 'out there' in the world. Wittgenstein thinks that this difference is part of the reason why propositions are so important for us. Propositions are vital to us because they enable us to communicate our thoughts to each other. My thoughts cannot be perceived by other people through the senses (because they are internal to me, within my head); but I *can* communicate them to others by means of propositions, since propositions are composed of signs (words) that others can perceive through their senses. I can communicate a thought to you by presenting you with a proposition that represents the same possible state also represented by my thought.

> In a proposition a thought finds an expression that can be perceived by the senses. (TLP 3.1)

Clearly, then, the relationship between thoughts and propositions is absolutely central to an exploration of language, communication and the mind.

Let us take a moment therefore to consider Wittgenstein's discussion of thoughts and of their relation to propositions. What we are about to cover will feel pretty familiar in some respects, since his conception of thought is closely similar to that of the proposition. For Wittgenstein, a thought is an arrangement of mental signs that represents one particular possible state. The possible state represented by a thought is the sense of that thought: thoughts, like propositions, are senseful. A thought with a particular sense can be communicated to other people by means of a proposition with the same sense. Imagine that, in the middle of a discussion about the travel arrangements of my friend Alice, I entertain the thought 'Alice is in London'. This thought can be expressed by means of a proposition: I can communicate my thought to you by presenting you with a proposition with the same sense – a proposition that represents the same possible state that is represented by the thought. Indeed, this is precisely how I *have* just expressed my thought: I have expressed it by means of the proposition 'Alice is in

London', a proposition expressed by means of words written in black ink on a white page. So, I communicate my thought to you by using an arrangement of (sense-perceptible) words to represent the same possible state that is represented by my thought: by presenting you with a proposition that has the same sense as my thought.

We use the perceptible sign of a proposition (spoken or written, etc.) as a projection of a possible situation.

The method of projection is to think of the sense of the proposition. (TLP 3.1)

Thoughts, like propositions, are arrangements of signs that represent possible states. Although thoughts and propositions are both arrangements of signs, it is clear that there are important distinctions between the concept of a thought and that of a proposition, notably differences in the type of signs that make them up. The mental signs that make up thoughts are not sense-perceivable; words are. But the similarities between the two concepts should also be clear. Most notably, both thoughts and propositions are arrangements of signs with a sense; they are arrangements of signs that represent particular possible states. Indeed, it is because thoughts and propositions are similar in this respect that propositions can express thoughts. One of the ways in which Wittgenstein emphasizes the similarities between propositions and thoughts is by noting that both of them are *'pictures'*.

Wittgenstein uses the term 'picture' in a very specific and unusual way. A picture, in this context, is any arrangement of signs that represents one particular possible state (one particular possible way in which reality could be). Pictures belong to different media: propositional pictures (propositions) belong to the medium of language, of words; thoughts, in turn, are pictures in a different medium, the medium of mental signs. The carrier medium in these two cases is different, but the internal, logical structure is closely similar. It is important to note that a picture for Wittgenstein is not necessarily something that can be perceived through the senses. The mental signs that make up thoughts cannot be perceived through the senses but they still form pictures. A picture, in his view, is therefore any representation of a possible state, in whatever medium.

A picture represents a possible situation in logical space. (TLP 2.202)

What a picture represents is its sense. (TLP 2.221)

So long as an arrangement of signs represents a particular possible state (so long as it has a sense), it is a picture – even if the signs in question cannot be perceived through the senses. Since a picture is essentially an arrangement of signs that represents a particular possible state, we could when reading the *Tractatus* simply substitute the word 'picture' for the word 'representation': a picture is a representation of a particular possible state.

So propositions and thoughts are both pictures, in Wittgenstein's view, albeit pictures conveyed in different media. In the *Tractatus*, Wittgenstein also discusses other types of pictures: representations of particular possible states that belong to other media, such as certain paintings and constructed models (for instance, a model train set). It is important to note that not all paintings or models count as pictures in this view. Paintings and models are arrangements of signs: coloured shapes on a canvas in the case of paintings; three-dimensional items in the case of models. But these arrangements of signs only count as pictures in Wittgenstein's sense when they are *used to represent a particular possible state*. The distinction we drew in Chapter 1 between a sentence and proposition is helpful here once again. Arrangements of coloured shapes on a canvas and arrangements of three-dimensional items, in and of themselves, are on a par with sentences: they are arrangements of signs that can be used to represent a *variety* of possible states. When they are used to represent a *particular* possible state, they become pictures with a sense. They are then on a par with propositions (rather than being merely on a par with sentences). Propositions, thoughts and other pictures are arrangements of signs that represent particular possible states: they are arrangements of signs with senses.

The mention of models is particularly important here. Indeed, the idea that propositions and thoughts are pictures (understood in this way) seems to have crystallized for Wittgenstein while reading an article in a magazine about the use of a model in a lawsuit about a car accident in Paris. Wittgenstein read that a model diorama consisting of miniature cars, roads, houses, etc. was used in court to represent the accident: the model was a representation (a *picture*) of a possible state of reality, in that it represented a particular (possible) car accident.[4] We can use this idea of the court proceedings to throw further light on Wittgenstein's notion of a picture. Imagine that, as part of a lawsuit, a (possible) car crash is represented in four different ways: by means of the written proposition 'the car struck the tree'; by means of the thought expressed by that proposition; by means of a model containing a miniature car and tree (as well as miniature houses, roads, etc.); and by means of a figurative painting of a car crashing into a tree. In this example, the proposition, the thought, the model and the painting are all *pictures*: they are all arrangements of signs that represent a possible state. In other words, they are all pictures with a *sense*. What's more, the way in which we have set up this example entails that these four pictures all have the *same* sense: they all represent the same possible state (the same possible car accident).

Wittgenstein suggests that, as pictures, the proposition, the thought, the model and the painting share some features in common. At the same time, the proposition and the thought, on the one hand, differ from the model and the painting, on the other, in at least one important respect. As we will now see, it is this key difference that renders propositions ideally suited for the communication of thoughts and representational models and paintings less ideal. Let us consider first the features that are shared in common by these four pictures – and then we will see what sets propositions and thoughts apart from the others.

At first glance, it seems difficult to see what the proposition 'the car struck the tree', the thought expressed by this proposition, the model and the painting could have in common. It is helpful here to remember that we are engaged here in a conceptual investigation: we are engaged in the process of trying to clarify the *concept* of a picture (the concept of a representation). More specifically, we are trying to clarify what is essential to this concept and what is not essential to it. Wittgenstein suggests that, in essence, a picture is an arrangement of signs that represents one specific possible state. The signs that make up the four pictures in our example are very different from each other: the signs that make up the written proposition are words in black ink on white paper; the signs that make up the thought are mental signs; the model consists of a miniature car, a miniature tree, and miniature roads and houses; the painting consists of painted coloured shapes. For all these differences, however, these four pictures share something in common: they all represent the same possible state, they all have the same sense. In order to see what this might involve, let us consider Wittgenstein's discussion of pictures in a little more detail.

Wittgenstein suggests that pictures are composite: they consist of elements – namely, of signs. Possible states (the possibilities represented by pictures) are also composite: they are made up of logical elements – elements which can ultimately be broken down into states of affairs consisting of simple meanings (or objects). Wittgenstein suggests that the arrangement of signs in a picture mirrors the arrangement of constituent elements in the possibility represented by that picture. In other words, the signs that make up a picture are arranged in a way that reflects the arrangement of elements in the possible state depicted by it. Wittgenstein calls this the 'structure' of the picture: a picture has a structure insofar as its arrangement of signs mirrors the arrangement of elements of the depicted possible state (TLP 2.15). Wittgenstein also suggests that the signs that make up a picture are correlated to the elements of the possible state represented by that picture. He calls these correlations the 'pictorial relationships' of the picture. So, a picture has pictorial relationships insofar as the signs that make it up are correlated or connected to the constituent elements of a possible state (TLP 2.1514).

In order to clarify Wittgenstein's notions of structure and of pictorial relationship, let us consider again three of the examples we were looking at above: the proposition 'the car struck the tree', the model and the painting. These pictures represent the same possible state, a possible state involving a certain car having collided with a tree. In these pictures, the word 'car', the miniature model car and the painted car shape are all correlated with the *car* element of the possible state. In turn, the word 'tree', the miniature model tree, and the painted tree shape are all correlated to the *tree* element of the possible state. These correlations constitute, in Wittgenstein's terminology, the pictorial relationships of these pictures. Wittgenstein suggests that the pictorial relationships of a picture go hand in hand with its structure. It is because these correlations are in place that these pictures mirror the arrangement of elements in this possible state; it is because these correlations (these pictorial relationships) are in place that these three pictures (the proposition, the painting and the model) can be said to have a *structure*, as pictures. If the signs that make up the proposition, the painting and the model were not correlated to the elements of a possible state – if they did not stand for the elements of a possible state – their arrangements would not represent anything. These signs regarded, respectively, as black markings on a piece of paper, as three-dimensional figures, as coloured shapes on canvas, might well be considered aesthetically pleasing – but they would not have *structures as pictures* without these correlations: they would not be pictures in the Wittgensteinian understanding at all.

Similarly, if the words, the painted shapes and the three-dimensional figures were correlated with the elements of some *other* possible state – if they stood for the logical elements of some other possibility – they would have different structures as pictures. They would, indeed, be different pictures with altogether different senses. For example, 'the car struck the tree', the painting and the model (considered merely as arrangements of signs) might, in a different lawsuit, be used to represent a different possible state – that of a different car striking a different tree, for example; or of a car-shaped publicity balloon drifting loose and getting tangled in a sculpture of a tree – there are many possibilities here.

As we saw before, this relates to the distinction we drew in Chapter 1 between a sentence and a proposition. We saw then that a sentence is an arrangement of words that can be used to represent a variety of possible states and that, when it is used to represent one particular possible state, it becomes a proposition with a sense. The same is true more generally of pictures. The painting and the model, regarded merely as arrangements of signs on a par with sentences, can be used to represent a variety of possible states. When they are used to represent a *particular* possible state, they become *pictures* in Wittgenstein's understanding of the term: they become representations with senses. Consider yet another example. Imagine that the sentence 'The car struck the tree', the painting and the model are used as part of a secret agent code to assert that two negotiating parties have come to a specific agreement regarding the handover of stolen missile blueprints. The signs in question (the words in the sentence, the painted shapes, the three-dimensional figures) would, in this scenario, be correlated to the elements of a very different possible state: they would stand for the logical elements of a possible state involving a particular negotiated agreement between spies. In this scenario, the arrangements of signs in the proposition, the painting and the model would mirror the arrangement of logical elements in this possible state – the one involving the spies and the stolen blueprints – instead of mirroring the arrangement of elements in the possible state involving a car (or a giant publicity balloon!) colliding against a tree.

We have just looked at Wittgenstein's notion of pictorial relationship and at his notion of structure. An arrangement of signs becomes a picture when these signs are correlated to the elements of a possible state; at that point, the picture acquires its structure – a structure that mirrors the structure of the represented possible state.

There is one other feature that is essential to all pictures, in Wittgenstein's view, a feature he calls 'logical form'. Logical form is the ability of a picture to be logically analyzed, ultimately, into elementary propositions consisting of names. In Chapter 1, we saw that, for Wittgenstein, it belongs to the very concept of proposition that propositions should ultimately be analyzable into elementary propositions consisting of names with simple, indestructible and unchangeable meanings (which he calls objects). We saw that this was a requirement, if sense was to be determinate. What we did not mention in Chapter 1 is that this analyzability into elementary propositions consisting of names is a feature, not only of propositions, but also of *all pictures*. All pictures – that is, all representations of particular possible states, all representations with a sense, no matter what form they take or in what medium they are expressed – are logically analyzable into elementary propositions consisting of names with simple meanings. If they were not, their senses would not be determinate; but indeterminate sense is no sense at all, according to the *Tractatus*. Without logical form, therefore, pictures would fail to be pictures with a sense at all (TLP 2.18).

According to Wittgenstein, then, all pictures possess logical form, if they are pictures at all. In other words, propositions, thoughts, paintings and models are all logically analyzable into elementary propositions made up of names. Wittgenstein suggests that this logical analysis is shared by a picture and the possible state represented by that picture: a picture that represents a possible state breaks down into elementary propositions that have as their senses the states of affairs into which the possible state itself breaks down. It is precisely because the picture and the possible state share their logical analyses that the picture is a picture of precisely *that* possible state. Logical form (logical analyzability) is therefore the absolute minimum that must be *shared* by a picture (in whatever medium) and the possible state it represents.

From this we can see how sense can be conveyed in an everyday manner not only by language (in all its variant forms) but also by models, paintings, hieroglyphs, street-signs, wiring diagrams, technical schematics and so on, so long as they are used to represent some possible state. They are all 'pictures' in Wittgenstein's understanding of the word. Even the missile blueprints in our spy example above can be used to convey sense to the dissident missile technicians eagerly awaiting their handover.

Having examined in a little more detail Wittgenstein's notion of a picture, we can return to the idea that thoughts too are pictures. According to Wittgenstein, thoughts are pictures consisting of mental signs. Like other pictures, a thought therefore possesses a structure, pictorial relationships and logical form: it is therefore ultimately analyzable down to the level of elementary propositions consisting of names with simple meanings. The arrangement of mental signs in a thought mirrors the arrangement of elements in the possible state depicted by that thought: this is the structure that the thought has, as a picture. In turn, the mental signs that constitute the thought are correlated with the logical elements of the possibility (of the possible state) represented by the thought. These correlations are the pictorial relationships of the thought. Finally, thoughts, like all pictures, are ultimately analyzable into elementary propositions consisting of names with simple, unchangeable and indestructible meanings: thoughts have logical form. It is the logical form of thoughts, their analyzability, that enables them to have determinate senses, and therefore senses at all.

So we have seen that *all* pictures possess structure, pictorial relationships and logical form, according to Wittgenstein. These three features are shared in common by propositions, thoughts, representational models and paintings, and all other representations of possible states. Propositions and thoughts differ from all other pictures in one important respect, however: they differ in what they have in common with the possible states they depict. We are about to see that propositions and thoughts are the most basic – perhaps we might say the purest, most elegant – method of representing possible states, and that this sets them apart from other pictures.

Wittgenstein suggests that there is an important difference between, on the one hand, propositions and thoughts and, on the other, other pictures (such as representational models and paintings). That difference has to do with the nature of the media in which these pictures are expressed. In order to see this, consider a little further the question of what is essential for a proposition, a thought, a painting and a model, to represent a possible state. What is the absolute minimum that these pictures must share with a possible state if they are to represent it? Well, we have just seen that, according to Wittgenstein, a picture (in whatever medium) must share the logical form of the possible state it represents if it is to represent it at all. That is, a picture of a possible state must be logically analyzable into elementary propositions that have as their senses the states of affairs into which the possible state itself breaks down. The logical analysis of the picture and that of the possible state must – as it were – run hand in hand. This is the absolute minimum that any picture, *in whatever medium*, must share with the possible state it represents in order to represent it at all: it is the *logical form* of all pictures.

In addition to this, there is something that paintings and models must share with the possible states they represent, if they are to represent them at all – something that is made necessary by the nature of their media, without which there would simply be no pictures (no representations) *in those media*. In the case of representational paintings, the additional requirement is that a painting must feature differences in colour tone: something that is exactly the same colour (the same tonality) all over cannot be used, *as a painting*, to represent a possible state. In the case of the models, this additional requirement is its three-dimensionality: something that isn't three-dimensional cannot be used, *as a model*, to represent a possible state. Something that isn't three-dimensional can, of course, be used to represent a possible state – but not *as a model* (not *in the medium of models*). For example, a two-dimensional page with words written in black ink can, of course, be used to represent a possible state – but it is not a model. Conversely, something that has no differences in colour tonality can, of course, be used to represent a possible state – but it is not a painting (e.g. a piece of paper that is exactly the same colour throughout can be used to represent a possible state – as, for instance, in Braille – but it cannot do so *as a painting*). Tonal differentiation is an essential aspect of pictures in the medium of painting: Wittgenstein puts this by saying that it is part of the *pictorial form* of paintings (TLP 2.17). Three-dimensionality is an essential aspect of pictures in the medium of models: it is part of the pictorial form of models. For Wittgenstein, the pictorial form of a picture is what a picture shares with the possible state it represents that enables the picture to represent it in its own particular medium. This is quite a lot to swallow, so let us break it down as follows.

The pictorial form of a picture is that aspect:
(a) that a picture *shares* with the possible state it represents, and
(b) that enables the picture to represent that possible state *in its own special medium*.

So, when a picture represents a possible state *as a painting*, it does so by virtue of the fact that both the picture and the possible state have tonal differentiation in common. This is part of the pictorial form of paintings. Similarly, when a picture represents a possible state *as a model*, it does so by virtue of the fact that the picture and the possible state have three-dimensionality in common. This is part of the pictorial form of models. In contrast, the notion of logical form can be presented in the following way.

The logical form of a picture is that aspect:
(a) that a picture *shares* with the possible state it represents, and
(b) that enables the picture to represent that possible state *regardless of its medium, in any way at all*.

As we saw before, logical form consists in logical analyzability. Wittgenstein suggests that some kinds of pictures have a pictorial form which is distinct from their logical form. Paintings and models are of this kind: their logical form is their logical analyzability; their pictorial forms involve, respectively, tonal differentiation and three-dimensionality. Propositions and thoughts, however, are not like this. What propositions and thoughts share with the possible states they depict – that which enables them to represent these states *in the particular way that they do (in their own special media)* – is *also* what enables them to represent *at all*: it is their logical analyzability into elementary arrangements of names. In this respect, propositions and thoughts are the purest, most elegant types of pictures there can be: they succeed in representing possible states purely by virtue of that which is necessary for representation to happen at all – purely by virtue of their logical analysability into elementary arrangements of names with simple, indestructible and unchangeable meanings. Thoughts and propositions don't need to resemble the possible states they represent in any further ways – they don't need to share with them tonal differentiation or three-dimensionality. Thoughts and propositions represent possible states purely by virtue of their logical form. Because of this, Wittgenstein suggests that thoughts and propositions are *strictly logical pictures*. Although all pictures are logical pictures (in that all pictures possess logical form), thoughts and propositions differ from all other pictures in that their pictorial form (such as it is) *is also their logical form:* propositions and thoughts do not possess a pictorial form distinct from their logical form (TLP 2.181; 2.182). Or, to put it another way, what propositions and thoughts share with the possible states they represent – that which enables them to represent these states in the particular way that they do – is also what all pictures share with the possible states they represent: their logical analyzability into arrangements of simples – that which enables them to represent at all. Let us call those pictures that are not strictly logical – such as paintings and models – iconic pictures, to differentiate them from thoughts and propositions.

So thoughts and propositions are strictly logical pictures. In this respect, they differ from iconic pictures, such as paintings and models. However, although thoughts and propositions coincide in this respect, there is also one important difference between them. Thoughts consist of mental signs that cannot be perceived through the senses. Propositions, by contrast, are expressed by means of signs (words) that *can* be perceived through the senses: through the sense of sight in the case of written words, through the sense of hearing in the case of spoken words, through the sense of touch in the case of Braille, etc. In *this* respect, propositions are closer to iconic pictures than they are to thoughts. After all, iconic pictures (e.g. the painting and the model we discussed above) consist of signs (coloured painted shapes and three-dimensional figures respectively) that can also be perceived through the senses. It is precisely this halfway status between thoughts and iconic pictures that renders propositions so important to the communication of thought. Propositions enable us to communicate thoughts to each other because they consist of perceptible signs (of words); at the same time, they are the ideal vehicles for the communication of thought because, unlike iconic pictures and like thoughts, they too are strictly logical pictures.

According to Wittgenstein, therefore, propositions are ideally suited for the communication of thought. I can communicate a thought to you by presenting you with a sense-perceptible (spoken, written, etc.) proposition, one that has the same sense as the thought in question. In other words, I can communicate a thought to you by presenting you with a proposition that affirms the same possible state that is represented by the thought. Pictures – including propositions – are such that, if you understand what is represented by the signs that make them up, you will understand what the picture as a whole represents. This means that you will be able to understand my proposition (and I will, therefore, be able to communicate my thought to you) so long as you understand the words that make up my proposition – regardless of whether or not you have ever encountered this particular proposition (this particular arrangement of words) before.

Before we bring this section to a close, it is worth mentioning one final point concerning Wittgenstein's use of the term 'thought'. For Wittgenstein, 'thought' is an umbrella term that covers many different types of mental representations (or mental pictures). For example, beliefs, memories and experiences (in particular, sensory experiences) are all types of thoughts, in his view. Beliefs, memories and experiences are all mental representations or mental pictures, according to Wittgenstein: they are all arrangements of mental signs that represent particular possible states. So, for instance: the experience of seeing that an apple is on the table involves mentally representing a particular possible state. So does remembering seeing this. Seeing, believing and remembering that the apple is on the table are all forms of thinking. As a result, they all involve having mental representations of a particular possible state – mental representations that can, in turn, be expressed by means of propositions with the same sense.

In Summary

- According to Wittgenstein, the concept of a picture is, essentially, that of an arrangement of signs that represents or asserts a possible state of reality. The signs in question can belong to a variety of media. Thoughts are pictures consisting of mental signs that cannot be perceived through the senses. Propositions and other pictures (such as representational paintings and

61

models) consist of signs that can be perceived through the senses (words in the case of propositions).

- Pictures are such that, if you know what the signs that make them up represent, you will be able to tell what the picture as a whole represents. All pictures possess a structure, pictorial relationships, a pictorial form and a logical form. A picture has a structure in that the arrangements of signs in the picture mirrors the arrangement of elements in the depicted possible state. The pictorial relationships of a picture consist in the correlation between these signs and the elements in the depicted state. Pictorial form is what is shared by the picture and the possible state that enables the picture to represent the state in its own particular medium: in the case of paintings, it involves tonal differentiation; in the case of models, three-dimensionality. Logical form, finally, is the absolute minimum that any picture must share with a possible state in order to represent it in any medium at all: it is its logical analyzability.
- Propositions and thoughts are strictly logical pictures. A strictly logical picture is one that does not have a pictorial form that is distinct from its logical form. In other words, it is such that:
  (a) the aspect shared by the picture and the possible state that enables the picture to represent the state *in its own particular medium* (pictorial form) is also
  (b) the aspect shared by the picture and the possible state it represents that enables the picture to represent the state *in any way (in any medium) at all* (logical form, logical analysability).
- Propositions – being strictly logical pictures (as thoughts are), while consisting (unlike thoughts) of sense perceptible signs – are the ideal vehicles for the communication of thought.

iii. THE CONCEPT OF SELF

For Wittgenstein, the concept of a thought is, essentially, that of a mental picture: a thought is an arrangement of mental signs that depicts or represents a particular possible state. Although the mental signs that make up a thought cannot be perceived through the senses, it is possible for us to communicate thoughts to each other by means of propositions. I can communicate a thought to you by presenting you with a proposition with the same sense as my thought. Propositions are ideally suited to the communication of thoughts since they are able to represent the same possible states represented by thoughts but to do so by means of signs (i.e. words) that other people can perceive. Thanks to propositions, thoughts become essentially communicable, in spite of the fact that they themselves consist of non-perceptible mental signs.

The question 'what is essential to the concept of thought?' was of special interest to Wittgenstein. There are, of course, many other important questions we could be asking about thoughts and thinking. For instance, we could be asking: what mechanism in the brain produces thought? Or, more specifically: what are the neurological processes that enable us to think? Alternatively, we could be asking questions about the types of thoughts we have. For instance, we could ask: how does depressive thinking manifest itself? What kinds of thoughts are characteristic of clinical depression? Questions such as these, though clearly important, do not fall under the remit of philosophy, according to Wittgenstein. Why not? Because answering them involves establishing the facts, it involves establishing what obtains in reality – and as we have seen, questions about facts are the purview of the natural sciences and not of philosophy, which concerns itself with concepts. Answering the first set of questions, for instance, involves establishing which brain mechanisms produce thought, *as a matter of fact, in reality*. The second involves establishing how, *as a matter of fact*, depressive thoughts manifest themselves *in reality*. Both questions would have to be answered by conducting empirical investigations into the facts, by gathering empirical information as to what takes place in reality. As we saw earlier, Wittgenstein believes philosophy to be a process that is distinct from such empirical investigations of the facts – so we can leave these thorny problems for neurologists and psychologists to solve.

The idea that philosophy and psychology are fundamentally distinct is central to Wittgenstein's notion of the self. The *Tractatus'* discussion of the self does not aim at establishing any psychological or neurological facts about selves: instead, it aims at clarifying the very concept of 'self' itself. From the point of view of philosophy, questions such as 'what am *I*?' or 'what is a self', are, in essence, conceptual questions. A philosopher asking these questions is really asking: what concept is at work when we speak of a self?

We have seen that for Wittgenstein, the aim of philosophy is to clarify concepts. We have also seen that, in Wittgenstein's view, philosophers in the past have done much the opposite – muddling and confusing instead of simplifying and clarifying. Instead of throwing light on concepts such as that of self, philosophers have too often succeeded only in obscuring them. For Wittgenstein, one philosopher was particularly culpable in this respect: his own mentor and friend, Bertrand Russell. Russell wrote repeatedly about the self, and had several changes of heart on this subject during his philosophical career. The *Tractatus* targets one of Russell's accounts of the self in particular – one developed by Russell in works such as 'On Denoting' and 'Knowledge by Acquaintance and Knowledge by Description', among others. In these writings, Russell presents selves as being essentially *simple*, in the sense of not being made up of elements. In Russell's view, a proposition such as 'I think that it is raining' should be understood as describing a relationship between something absolutely simple and indivisible (the simple self, the *I*) and a composite thought (the thought 'It is raining'). One of the implications of Russell's view is that simple selves are the legitimate subject matter of psychology. In other words, Russell's view implies that part of the aim of psychology should be to investigate the notion of a simple self that thinks or entertains thoughts. Psychology would, in this view, be the study of simple selves and their particular relations to (complex) thoughts. Wittgenstein is, of course, happy with the idea that thoughts are complex; after all, he suggests that a thought is a *complex* arrangement of mental signs. It is with the idea that selves might be *simple* that he has a problem. Wittgenstein sees Russell's notion of simple self and his views concerning its role in psychology as being profoundly mistaken. Let us see why he thinks this.

For Wittgenstein, psychology – properly understood – is one of the natural sciences. As such, it focuses on empirical investigations that aim at providing us with true descriptions of the facts. Empirical investigations rely on experience: they involve experiencing reality and thereby establishing what obtains, as a matter of fact, in reality. Empirical investigations involve two main types of experience, according to Wittgenstein: sense experience (i.e. perception through the five senses of sight, hearing, touch, smell and taste) and introspective experience (or introspection, namely the process of – as it were – looking inside one's own mind). Imagine a psychologist trying to establish the real psychological state of a patient. In order to establish this, the psychologist would carry out an empirical investigation that relied on both sense experience and introspective experience. The psychologists would, through the sense of sight, observe the behaviour of the patient; she would listen to what the patient says; and she would look inside her own mind in order to monitor her own beliefs and memories relating to the case.

Psychologists carry out empirical investigations into selves with a view to establishing the facts about these selves. Empirical investigations rely crucially on experiences, beliefs and memories. Now, as we saw earlier, experiencing, believing and remembering all involve mentally representing possible states for Wittgenstein – they all involve having mental pictures of possible states. If selves were simple, however, it would not be possible to represent them – either mentally or in language. Something that is simple cannot be *described* by means of propositions – that would be rather like trying to build a brick up out of houses. Nor can it be pictured in experience, beliefs, memories or thoughts (or any other type of 'picture'). If something is genuinely simple, then it cannot be represented. But this, in Wittgenstein's view, entails that it cannot be experienced, believed, remembered or thought.

In Chapter 1, we saw that Tractarian simple objects cannot be described: they can only be named. If selves were simple, as Tractarian objects are, we would not be able to provide any descriptions of them: we would only be able to name them. But the task of a psychologist is to *describe* reality, not to merely *name* bits of it. Naming is an important activity, of course, but it is not the purpose of the natural sciences, in Wittgenstein's view: natural scientists aim to describe how reality works, and that can only be done by constructing propositions (statements about reality) – it cannot be done simply by naming. This is an idea we discussed in Chapter 1, when we considered the difference between the meanings of names and the senses of propositions. As part of that discussion, we saw that a scientist trying to give a description of our universe could not limit herself to naming the contents of that universe and listing these names. In order to describe our universe, it is essential to put forward full propositions rather than just lists of names. Since one of the aims of psychology is to provide us with true, factual descriptions of selves, Russell's concept of simple self cannot be the genuine subject matter of psychology.

So according to Wittgenstein, simple selves are not the legitimate subject matter of psychology. Instead, psychology should be regarded as the study of composite – not simple – selves, or minds. A mind, in this context, is basically a complex arrangement of thoughts. My mind consists in a complex arrangement of thoughts; my mind differs from your mind in that at least some of the thoughts that make it up are different from the thoughts that make up your mind. Minds conceived of in this way are complex and therefore describable by means of propositions. To describe a mind is to describe the array of (complex) thoughts that make it up. It is because minds are complex that they can be studied in experience by psychologists. A psychologist can examine her own mind (understood as the collection of her thoughts) by means of introspection; and she can study other people's minds by examining, by means of sense perception, the propositions they utter, which express their thoughts.

For Wittgenstein, the notion of the self that is the legitimate subject matter of psychology is that of the composite mind, not that of a simple, thinking self. Psychology, properly understood, is the study of composite minds and composite thinking. It aims at providing us with true descriptions of the facts about minds and thinking, and it does so by studying minds through experience (in sense-perception and introspection). The notion of a simple self is not a valid psychological notion of the self, because it simply does not fit with the role and purposes of psychology. The appropriate psychological notion of the self is that of the composite mind: the mind, understood in this way, is certainly the legitimate subject matter of psychology. This notion of composite mind is not, of course, important only to psychologists. Whenever, in more ordinary situations, I speak or think of my self or of other selves, I am representing complex minds (TLP 5.54–5.5423). If selves were simple as Russell suggests, it would not just be psychologists who would be unable to speak or think of them: no-one could.

In Summary

- Russell is mistaken in arguing that the legitimate subject matter of psychology is the notion of a simple self that thinks or entertains thoughts.
- In Wittgenstein's view, this supposedly psychological notion of the self does not fit with the aims and methods of psychology.

Psychology, being a natural science, aims at providing us with true descriptions of (i.e. true propositions about) selves. These descriptions are based on particular experiences of selves (experiences in sense perception and introspection). The simple selves posited by Russell could not be represented in language or in thought. Hence, they could not be described by means of propositions: they could only be named.

– The notion of the self which is the legitimate subject matter of psychology is not that of a simple, thinking self, but that of composite mind: the mind understood as a complex array of thoughts. Selves, understood in this way, are describable in language and can be experienced, and thought of precisely because they are complex.

iv. SOLIPSISM AND THE SELF

According to Wittgenstein, the notion of simple, thinking self posited by Russell (and other philosophers before him) has had a highly pernicious effect in philosophy. One of its most damaging consequences has been that of encouraging a philosophical doctrine I will call 'restrictive solipsism'. Restrictive solipsism suggests that there is something of special philosophical importance about my self (about *I*), as opposed to other selves: my self (*I*) can be regarded as restricting (or conditioning) the range of things that exist. There are several versions of restrictive solipsism, but Wittgenstein is especially interested in one of them: the view that only I and those things that I can possibly think of exist. According of this version of solipsism, nothing exists except for I and those things I can possibly think of. In other words, in this view, the range of things that exist is restricted or conditioned by my self and by my possible thoughts.

Although on the surface restrictive solipsism might appear implausible, it is nevertheless a deeply entrenched problem in philosophy. It is a problem in that it runs counter our common sense intuitions about what might exist but is frustratingly difficult to disprove or argue against. It is deeply entrenched also in that it is supported by philosophical arguments that have traditionally been regarded as very difficult to overturn. Typically, the arguments for restrictive solipsism focus on the idea that if something cannot possibly be thought of, there is no reason to assume that it exists and we should indeed assume that it does not. Consider, for instance, the following argument, which we will call (RS):

(RS)
(a) Things that cannot possibly be thought of do not exist.
(b) It is not possible to think of other selves
(c) I can think of my self (of *I*), as well as of other things

Conclusion:
Only I and those other things I can possibly think of exist.

Although this style of argument is quite common in traditional philosophy, it can take one aback at first; so let us consider each step in a little detail. Step (a) turns on the idea that, if it is *absolutely* impossible (for *any* creature) to think of something – if that thing is by its nature radically unthinkable or inconceivable, if it is not a possible object of thought *at all* – then there is no reason to assume that such a thing exists. In that case we should assume that the thing in question does *not* exist. This is the idea encapsulated in step (a): things that cannot possibly be thought of do not exist. The argument proceeds in step (b) to say that it is not possible to think of *other* selves: the nature of selves is such that it is impossible – for any creature – to think of *other* selves; other selves are not a possible object of thought for any creature. The argument then moves on to step (c): I can however think of *my own self* (as well as of other things).

These three steps together lead to restrictive solipsism – that is, to the conclusion that only *I* and *those things I can possibly think of* exist. The three steps of (RS) and its conclusion are all problematic in many respects. Indeed, the *Tractatus* offers several criticisms of (RS). In what follows, we will look at one of them in detail.

Wittgenstein suggests that arguments such as (RS) are predicated on one particular and conceptually confused understanding of *self*. Indeed, if we understood 'self' in (RS) as standing for composite *mind*, then (b) would simply not be very convincing. After all, it is perfectly possible to think of other people's *minds*: we often think and speak of other people's minds in the context of our ordinary lives, as do psychologists within their particular branch of the natural sciences. This is totally unmysterious for Wittgenstein (at least at this stage in his career), since minds, in his view, are complex collections of thoughts – and being complex, they can of course be represented in both language and in thought. In Tractarian terms it is therefore entirely possible to think of other people's minds: I can describe someone else's mind in language, by means of propositions; and I can also represent it in thought, I can think of it. For Wittgenstein, minds are complex arrangements, and, being complex, they are perfectly representable in language and in thought.

The idea that it is not possible to think of other selves – step (b) of (RS) – can only get off the ground if one assumes a different notion of self: the self understood, not as a complex collection of thoughts, but as the simple thing that thinks or entertains thoughts and that is as it were 'impenetrable' to other selves. In other words, the argument for restrictive solipsism can only proceed to step (b) if one takes for granted Russell's notion of the simple thinking self. It is precisely for this reason that Wittgenstein regards Russell's notion of simple thinking self as fuelling the argument for restrictive solipsism: (RS) breaks down immediately in (b) *unless* one assumes from the start that this very specific and limited notion of the simple thinking self is at work in it.

In fact, according to Wittgenstein, the argument for restrictive solipsism breaks down even if we allow Russell's simple self house-room. Step (c) suggests that it is possible for me to think of my self; but if the notion of self at work here is Russell's notion, then as we have seen, *it is not possible for me to think of my self.* Thinking of my self would involve mentally representing something that is simple. And, according to Wittgenstein, simple things cannot be represented in language or in thought. For something to be representable, and therefore thinkable, it needs to be complex; my self if we understand it as a simple thing in Russell's terms, is not something that I or anyone else can think of. Hence, just as it is impossible to think of other simple selves, it is impossible (for me or anyone else) to think of my self understood as a simple, thinking thing. I can think of my self understood as a composite mind (as a collection of thoughts) – but I cannot think of myself understood as a simple thinking thing. Indeed, Wittgenstein notes that, when one looks inside one's own mind (when one introspects), one never finds anything like a simple thinking self. When I look inside my mind, I only ever come across thoughts; I never come across some supposedly simple self somehow sitting in there having those thoughts: I have no experience (no mental representation) of such a simple self (TLP 5.633).

(RS) is therefore doomed from the start as an argument for restrictive solipsism. If one assumes that the notion of self at work in (RS) is that of a composite mind, the argument falls flat in step (b): for, in Wittgenstein's view, it is clearly possible under such circumstances to think of other people's selves. If, on the contrary, one assumes that the notion of self at work in (RS) is Russell's notion of a simple thinking self, then the argument fails in step (c). For it is just as impossible for me to think of (i.e. to mentally represent) my self as a simple thinking thing as it is for me to think of others understood as simple thinking selves.

> There is no such thing as the subject that thinks or entertains ideas. (TLP 5.631)

> Here it can be seen that solipsism, when its implications are followed out strictly, coincides with pure realism. The self of solipsism shrinks to a point without extension [. . .]. (TLP 5.64)

In this way Wittgenstein shows restrictive solipsism to be a house of cards lacking a foundation. Even using Russell's superficially beguiling notion of the simple self, the argument fails to hold. Restrictive solipsism was never a genuine philosophical problem. It only *appeared* to be a problem because the underlying concepts had not been clarified. This lack of clarity led to a surface argument (RS) that appeared complex and intractable, but which was *really* only muddled and confused. By applying what Wittgenstein sees as the true purpose of philosophy – that of clarification of concept – to the basic starting points of the argument, we can reveal it for what it is: a mistake from the beginning.

In Summary

- Russell's notion of simple, thinking self has had a detrimental effect in philosophy, in that it has helped fuel the theory of restrictive solipsism.
- Wittgenstein is interested in one particular version of restrictive solipsism: the view that only I and those other things I can think of exist. (RS) provides an argument for this view.
- (RS) requires the notion of simple thinking self, in order to get off the ground in step (b); but, if it does presuppose this notion

of the self, it collapses in step (c). It collapses because it is as impossible for me to think of myself understood as a simple thinking self as it is for me to think of other selves understood in this way. (RS) fails because the notion of the self that makes step (b) acceptable (that of simple, thinking thing), makes step (c) unacceptable and therefore makes it impossible for the argument to proceed to its conclusion.

- Wittgenstein rejects, in the *Tractatus*, the notion of simple thinking self and any restrictive solipsism based on this notion.

v. CONCLUSION

Wittgenstein's discussion of thought and the self plays a major role in the *Tractatus*. It helps to illustrate, in a very direct manner, how the process of conceptual clarification advocated by the *Tractatus* can help to resolve deeply entrenched philosophical problems. In this particular instance, clarifying the concept of thought gives Wittgenstein the ammunition he needs in order to dismantle one of the central arguments for restrictive solipsism.

In the *Tractatus*, Wittgenstein argues that a thought is, in essence, an arrangement of mental signs that represents a particular possible state – a mental picture. Although the mental signs that make up thoughts cannot be perceived through the senses, thoughts are nevertheless essentially communicable: we can communicate thoughts to each other in that we can express them by means of propositions. Propositions are perfectly suited to the task of communicating thoughts. Unlike thoughts, they consist of signs that can be perceived through the senses (of words). Like thoughts, they are strictly logical pictures. For this reason, propositions can represent the very same states represented by thoughts, and do so, just as thoughts do, purely by virtue of their logical analyzability. This intimate relation between propositions and thoughts means that my thoughts can be rendered accessible to others: I can communicate a thought to you simply by presenting you with a proposition with the same sense as my thought, in spite of the fact that my thought consists of signs that you cannot perceive through the senses.

Having clarified the essential features of the concept of thought, Wittgenstein examines the concept of a self. In so doing, he introduces the notion of a composite mind. A mind, in this context, is a complex collection of thoughts (of mental pictures). The self, understood in this way as a complex mind, is describable by means of propositions and can be examined in experience (either via sense perception or via introspection). In this respect, it fits perfectly with the aims and methods of the natural science of psychology. According to Wittgenstein, it is this concept of the self (the concept of a complex mind) that should be regarded as the legitimate subject matter of psychology.

Wittgenstein draws a contrast between this concept of the self understood as a complex mind and Russell's notion of the simple thinking self. Wittgenstein finds Russell's approach to the self profoundly misguided. The Russellian simple thinking self cannot be the legitimate subject matter of psychology. Indeed, the notion of a simple self does not fit with the aims and methods of psychology. A simple self could be neither described in language nor examined in experience. But psychology, being a natural science, aims at describing the world by means of propositions and at doing so on the basis of empirical investigations (investigations based on experience). Wittgenstein sees Russell as mistaken in implying that this notion of simple thinking self is central to psychology. Similarly, Russell is also mistaken in implying that this notion of simple thinking self is at work when we speak of selves in our ordinary lives: if selves were simple, we would not be able to speak or think of them at all.

For Wittgenstein, the Russellian notion of a simple self is profoundly damaging to philosophy. It is damaging in that it is superficially attractive, and helps to fuel the problematic philosophical doctrine of restrictive solipsism – a doctrine which is also superficially convincing until examined from the ground up in a rigourous way. In the *Tractatus*, Wittgenstein uses his discussion of thought and of the mind to show that restrictive solipsism cannot in fact be defended.

CHAPTER 3

LOGIC AND ETHICS

i. INTRODUCTION

There is little doubt that Wittgenstein regarded the *Tractatus* as having a fundamental ethical dimension. Shortly after finishing it he wrote to Ludwig von Ficker – with whom he was in correspondence about the possibility of publishing the book – a letter in which he insisted that 'the point of the book is an ethical one'.[5] This is likely to come as a surprise to anyone who reads it, however. For, certainly on the surface, the *Tractatus* appears to have very little to do with those questions traditionally regarded as central to ethics – questions such as 'what is goodness?' or 'when is an action right?'. Only a minute proportion of the book touches upon themes that could be regarded as connected to ethics, notably some of the entries beginning with 6.4ff and 6.5ff. In addition, those remarks that do appear to relate to ethics are, for the most part, negative in character: they concentrate on what ethics *is not like*, rather than on what ethics *is*. Given all this, it seems very surprising that, in writing to von Ficker, Wittgenstein should have chosen to highlight precisely the area of ethics as being central to his book. The letter is also surprising in that it reveals a very unusual conception of ethics: it suggests that the *Tractatus* succeeds in having an ethical point precisely by virtue of the fact that it is mostly silent about ethics. Wittgenstein writes:

[. . .] the point of the book is an ethical one. I once wanted to include in the preface a sentence that is now actually not there, but that I will write to you now since it might be a key for you: I wanted to write that my book consists of two parts: of the one that is present here and of everything I have *not* written. Precisely this second part is the important one. For the ethical is delimited as it were from the inside by my book; and I am convinced that *strictly* speaking it can ONLY be delimited in this way. In short I think: everything of which *many* nowadays are blethering, I have defined in my book by being silent about it [. . .] I would recommend you to read the *preface* and the *conclusion* since they express the point most directly.[6]

In Wittgenstein's view, it is because the *Tractatus* refrains from 'blethering' on the subject of ethics that it succeeds in having a genuine ethical dimension. Silence is crucial in ethics. Why should this be? Well, according to Wittgenstein, it is simply not possible to speak of ethics: ethics cannot be put into language, in that it cannot be described by means of propositions.

So it is impossible for there to be propositions of ethics.
Propositions can express nothing that is higher. (TLP 6.42)

It is clear that ethics cannot be put into words. (TLP 6.421)

The view that ethics cannot be put into words gives rise to an obvious tension, however – one that lies at the very heart of the *Tractatus*. For, if ethics cannot be put into words, how can a *book* – something that is, after all, made up of words – have an ethical point? In what way can an arrangement of words have an ethical dimension, if there can be no 'propositions of ethics'? As we will see towards the end of this chapter, the key to dissolving this puzzle lies in noting the intimate connection that exists between logic and ethics for Wittgenstein. Before we are able to turn to this issue, though, it is important to consider Wittgenstein's attitude towards traditional ethics. We will be looking at this in the next section; we will then be in a position to consider Wittgenstein's views on the relation between logic and ethics and the whole issue of the ethical point of the *Tractatus*.

In Summary

– Wittgenstein claims that 'the point [of the *Tractatus*] is an ethical one' (Letter to von Ficker).[7]
– This claim is surprising given how little of the text of the *Tractatus* explicitly touches upon ethics.

– The claim is made all the more mysterious by the fact that Wittgenstein suggests, in the *Tractatus*, that ethics cannot be put into words: if ethics cannot be put into words, how can the point of his book – which is, after all, made up of words – be an ethical one?

ii. TRADITIONAL ETHICS AND THE INFLUENCE OF SCHOPENHAUER

In writing the *Tractatus*, Wittgenstein offers a critique of what he regards as the traditional approach to ethics. The traditional conception of ethics criticized by Wittgenstein has three central features. First and rather basically, it assumes that ethics can be put into words – indeed, it assumes that part of the aim of the moral philosopher is to provide us with moral theories couched in language. Secondly, the traditional approach assumes that the notion of action is central to ethics and that at least part of the aim of moral philosophy is to determine when actions are right and when they are wrong. Finally, the traditional approach holds that at least some degree of freedom is necessary for morality to be possible. Let us look at each of these ideas in turn in order to gain a clearer view of the position that Wittgenstein opposes.

Traditional ethics, as they are understood by Wittgenstein, assumes first of all that it is possible to describe ethical views by means of propositions. In this traditional view, moral philosophers spend their time coming up with theories that consist precisely of such 'ethical propositions'. Having said this, it is worth noting that the question of the extent to which ethics can be put into words was already in the air when Wittgenstein arrived in Cambridge in 1911. A few years before, G. E. Moore – who would become one of Wittgenstein's mentors in Cambridge – had published *Principia Ethica*. In this major work of ethics, Moore argues that goodness is a property that cannot be defined by means of words. According to Moore, it is not possible to *say* what goodness is: goodness is a *simple* property; for this reason it is not possible to give a definition of it.

Although Moore's view limits the range of things that can be said in ethics – in that it rules out the possibility of defining goodness – it does not go as far as suggesting that there can be no ethical propositions whatsoever. Indeed, while the property of goodness cannot be defined, it is compatible with Moore's view to say that certain things *are* good – that they possess this property. The moral philosopher can, in this view, work at clarifying which things are good (which things happen to possess this simple, indefinable property of goodness) and which are not. Moral philosophers might, for instance, discuss whether happiness is good (whether happiness possesses the property of goodness), whether knowledge is good, etc. The first feature of the traditional conception of ethics that Wittgenstein criticizes is therefore that ethics can – at least to some extent – be put into words. In this respect, Moore belongs to the traditional camp. For although Moore believed that there could be no ethical propositions that defined goodness, he nevertheless believed that other types of ethical propositions *were* possible. It is this willingness to engage with some aspects of ethics within a framework of language with which Wittgenstein takes issue.

The second aspect of the traditional approach opposed by Wittgenstein is that it places a great emphasis on the notion of *action*: it holds action to be at the heart of ethical debate. It is important to clarify what is meant by 'action' in this context. Here, actions are distinguished from mere physical movement in that actions are performed on the basis of motives (or reasons, or intentions). For instance, there is a difference between my walking across the park because I want to go home quickly and the fastest route is through the park and my being blown across the park by a gale-force wind. In both cases, I end up physically moving across the park. However, whereas in the former case I perform an *action*, in the latter I do not: I cannot be said to be *acting* if I am merely being blown about by a strong wind.

The difference between these two cases lies in part in what lies behind my physical movement across the park. In the first case, I act on the basis of a motive (or a reason): I have the desire to go home quickly and the belief that walking across the park is the fastest route home; the combination of the two motivates me (or gives me a reason) to walk across the park. In this case, I walk across the park, as it were, of my own volition. My action of walking across the park comes about as a result of something that is in my mind: a desire and a belief of mine. In the second case, my physical movement across the park is not the product of something that can, in any way, be described as 'in my mind': my movement is brought about by a force altogether external to me, by the force of the wind. Actions, understood in this way as incorporating motives or reasons, are central to the traditional ethical approach that Wittgenstein criticizes. Kant and Schopenhauer – both of whom are widely recognized as having exerted a major influence on Wittgenstein's views – argue that the goodness or badness of a motive (or reason) is of paramount importance when it comes to deciding whether a resulting action is right or wrong. Although their views differ in major respects, both agree that an action is right if it is brought about by a good motive and wrong if it results from a bad one. As we will soon see, Wittgenstein does not accept that ethics should be primarily concerned with sorting out the difference between right and wrong actions. In fact, he feels that this emphasis on action indicates a fundamental misunderstanding of what ethics is.

The third aspect of the approach to ethics opposed by Wittgenstein involves the notion of freedom. The traditional approach sees freedom as fundamental to ethics, to the extent that there can be no ethics (in particular, no moral responsibility) without it. The idea, in a nutshell, is that it is simply not appropriate to hold someone morally responsible for their actions if their actions are not free. Imagine that I promise to be home at a certain time, for instance because my house mate is seriously ill and needs my help. If I break my promise because a gale-strong wind blows me across the park, then I should not be held morally responsible for breaking my promise. It makes little sense to view me as a morally bad person or to *blame* me under these circumstances. Since I was not free to act on this occasion, I should not be held morally responsible (I should not be blamed) for breaking my promise. Freedom, in the traditional view, is central to morality. Indeed, if human beings turned out not to be free, this would entail that they were totally incapable of morality: if human beings are not free, it is not appropriate to speak of them as morally good or bad persons, or to hold them responsible for the rightness or wrongness of their actions. In that case, we would to all intents and purposes have to give up on ethics.

Although there are several definitions among moral philosophers as to what constitutes 'freedom', one of the most influential and widespread definitions suggests that freedom has primarily to do with the question of 'ultimate origination'. In this view, my action is free if it ultimately originates in me: if I am its ultimate source. If I am blown across the park by a strong wind, I cannot be said to be free in so doing. My moving across the park is not an instance of a free action, because it is brought about by something external to me: I am not the ultimate source or the ultimate originator of this movement – the wind is. The idea that freedom generally (and this notion of freedom in particular – freedom as ultimate origination) is a prerequisite of ethics is rejected by Wittgenstein, as we will see shortly.

Wittgenstein's approach to ethics, then, is unusual to say the least in that it runs counter three major strands in traditional ethics: the idea that ethics can be put into words, the idea that action and motivation are central to moral philosophy, and the idea that freedom is a condition of moral responsibility and, more broadly, of morality itself. All of these three strands are present in various degrees in Schopenhauer's main work: *The World as Will and Representation*. Schopenhauer's influence on Wittgenstein is beyond doubt. In a 1931 diary entry, Wittgenstein gives a list of the thinkers that had exercised the greatest influence over his philosophical work – a list in which Schopenhauer is placed third. Wittgenstein read Schopenhauer for the first time when he was a schoolboy, and then again before he began on the *Tractatus*. That he was much taken with Schopenhauer's approach to ethics is obvious when one reads Wittgenstein's *Notebooks 1914–1918*. The *Notebooks* is the main precursor of the *Tractatus*: in this earlier text, Wittgenstein rehearses and develops many of the lines of thought that find their final expression in the *Tractatus*. The *Notebooks*' passages on the subject of ethics show that Wittgenstein was, in the run up to writing the *Tractatus*, much preoccupied with various aspects of Schopenhauer's moral philosophy. Indeed, they show that Wittgenstein went as far as accepting some of Schopenhauer's insights in the years just before the writing of the *Tractatus*. The evidence suggests, however, that by the time he came to write the *Tractatus*, Wittgenstein had rejected Schopenhauer's central stance on ethics. In particular, he had come to reject the three views we discussed above. Part of Wittgenstein's aim, in writing the *Tractatus*, is to present an alternative to Schopenhauer's ethics and, in particular, to these three views. In order to understand the ethical dimension of the *Tractatus*, it is therefore important to spend a moment considering what Schopenhauer had to say – the background view against which Wittgenstein was reacting.

Schopenhauer's moral philosophy originates from a very particular understanding of the world. According to Schopenhauer, the world we perceive through our senses is strongly deterministic. There are two key elements to this idea. The first is that everything in the world is brought about by a prior cause; indeed, everything that exists and everything that happens in the world is the product of a long chain of causes and effects, dating back to the beginning of existence. The second is the idea that causation involves a *necessary connection*. Causation is such that, if A causes B, then, if A obtains, it is absolutely *impossible* for B not to obtain too. If A occurs, then B is inevitable: there is no possibility of B not occurring.

Schopenhauer believes that human beings are subject to this strong causal determinism, in so far as they are part of the world. This means, in particular, that human beings are mistaken in believing that their actions are ever free. Let us take again the example of my walking across the park in order to get home as fast as possible. We saw above that the motive behind my action of walking across the park involved my desire to be home as fast as possible. We also saw that freedom, in Schopenhauer's view, is primarily to do with origination: my action is free if I am its ultimate source; it is unfree if it is brought about by something external to me.[8] For Schopenhauer, human actions cannot be free, because they are brought about by desires – and desires are themselves subject to causal determination by outside forces. My desire to be home as fast as possible is the effect of a prior cause, which is itself the effect of a prior cause, etc. The chain of causes and effects that gives rise to my desire to be home as fast as possible involves things that are external to me. For instance, in this example, my desire to be home as fast as possible is caused by my desire to help my ill friend; the latter desire is (at least in part) the result of the upbringing that my parents gave me; their desire to bring me up in this particular way was brought about by the upbringing that their parents gave them, and so on. My desire to get home as fast as possible is the product of a long chain of causes and effects that does not originate in me, but which stretches back to way before I was even born. I am not the ultimate source of this desire: I am not the ultimate source of the motive behind my action. Since my action does not have me as its ultimate source, it cannot be regarded as a free action. The chain of causes that leads to my crossing the park does not start with me: I am not its ultimate originator. My sense of being in control, the sense that *I* caused or brought about this action is thus, in fact, an illusion. Indeed, in Schopenhauer's view, I have no genuine control over my action. My action is subject to causal necessity: given the complex chain of causes and effects that produced it, my action was inevitable – it would have been impossible for me to act in a different way.

According to Schopenhauer, everything *in* the world – whether it is mental (e.g. my desire) or physical (e.g. the movement of my legs when walking across the park) – is subject to this strong causal determinism. In so far as they are part of the world, human beings are therefore unfree. That said, Schopenhauer does not believe that human beings are *totally* unfree; and he manages this apparent contradiction by suggesting that there is a part of us that does not fall within the world of causal determinism. Human beings are special creatures for Schopenhauer; this can be seen most clearly when one considers his discussion of what he calls the 'will'.

According to Schopenhauer, human beings are endowed with two kinds of will. The first he calls the phenomenal will. The phenomenal will is that part of the will that is *in* the world and is therefore subject to causal determinism. This is the will understood quite ordinarily as our psychological desires, wants and wishes: the will that is involved in motivating action, like my motivation to cross the park. This phenomenal will *is* subject to causation; as such, it is incapable of freedom. This means that *what desires I do have* are the product of a long chain of causes and effects that predates me and that is therefore external to me. The fact that I have the desire to help my friend (rather than the desire to harm her) is the product of my upbringing, of my parents' own upbringing, etc. Someone else's desire to harm their friends (rather than help them) is the result of a different chain of causes and effects, involving their upbringing, their parents' upbringing, etc. So my phenomenal will is subject to causal determinism in that it would not have been possible for me to have desires other than the ones I have, given the complex chain of causes and effects that produced me.

However, human beings are also endowed with a different kind of will, which Schopenhauer calls the 'noumenal will'. The noumenal will is an aspect of human beings that is *not* inside the causally determined world. Because it is not *in* the world, the noumenal will is not subject to causation. As such, it is free in a way that the phenomenal will could never be. The noumenal will is the only possible source of freedom for human beings. The freedom it enables us to have is, in some ways, very limited; but if we believe Schopenhauer, it is the only freedom possible for human beings and it is fundamental to leading a good life.

So, we have just seen that the noumenal will is not subject to causation: it is not part of the complex network of causes and effects that makes up the world. For this reason, the noumenal will has no causal powers over those things that are subject to causal determination. In particular, I cannot (noumenally) *cause* my desires to be different from what they are. If my noumenal will *could* do this, then my actions could be said to be free after all. In this scenario, I could, for instance, cause myself to switch desires: I could replace my desire to get home as fast as possible with a desire to go to the pub, which in turn would cause me to perform a different action – that of walking to the pub, rather than that of going home. The noumenal will has no causal powers, however; so my desire to return home quickly remains the same. What the noumenal will does offer, though, is the ability to alter my *attitude* towards these desires that I have. This, in Schopenhauer's view, is what constitutes human freedom.

What kind of freedom is made possible by the noumenal will, then? According to Schopenhauer, there are two possible attitudes we can adopt when confronted with our desires: we can give in to our impulse to desire; or we can attempt to abandon our desires. The former attitude is that of someone who holds on to their desires, who concentrates on them and on the expectation of their fulfilment, and who is therefore desperately unhappy when they are not satisfied. Schopenhauer tells us that this attitude makes for a bad, unhappy life. The latter attitude is that of someone who lets go of their desires, who recognizes their futility. Adopting this attitude involves recognizing that my desires are not genuinely *mine* (since they result from a chain of causes and effects that predates me) and also that whether or not they are fulfilled is something over which I have absolutely no control. This attitude of abandoning one's desires is what Schopenhauer says makes for a happy life. Although we have no control over the world, and therefore cannot be said to freely choose what takes place in the world, we have freedom in that we can decide which of these two attitudes to adopt: we can hold on to the illusion of control and carve out a fundamentally unhappy life for ourselves, or we can let go of this illusion, by letting go of our desires. Happiness for Schopenhauer does not consist in satisfying our desires but in abandoning desire altogether, and the happy life is the life of those who have succeeded in this aim. This is also the good life: it is good (*morally* good) in so far as it rests on a (noumenally) free choice between two attitudes – the attitude of holding on to desire (to the phenomenal will) and the attitude of letting go of it. Although we may not think this is much of a free choice, Schopenhauer's view is that it is the only one we have actually got – and what is more, it is our only hope for happiness (the happiness that comes from abandoning desire).

In Summary

– Wittgenstein regards traditional ethics as mistakenly advocating the following views:
  (a) Ethics can be put into words.
  (b) The notions of action and motive are at the heart of ethics.
  (c) There are no ethics, and no moral responsibility, without freedom and choice.
  Although Wittgenstein was an admirer of Schopenhauer and was in tune with some aspects of his ethics, he also regarded the latter as mistakenly embracing all three of these views.
– According to Schopenhauer, the world is strongly deterministic: everything in the world is subject to causal necessity. We are not the ultimate causal source of anything that happens in the world: we are not free with respect to (and in particular we do not freely choose) anything that takes place in the world. Our own actions and desires are the result of chains of causes and effects that predate us and are external to us.
– For Schopenhauer, human beings possess a phenomenal and a noumenal will. The phenomenal will (characterized by one's desires, wants, wishes, etc.) is part of the world. As such, it is subject to causation and therefore unfree. The noumenal will, in contrast, is not part of the world: it is not subject to causation and, for this reason, is the only possible source of human freedom.
– In Schopenhauer's view, human beings are only free insofar as their noumenal will allows for it. Although the noumenal will cannot alter what takes place in the world, it does provide us with the freedom to choose what attitude to take towards the world. In particular, it enables us to freely determine what attitude to take towards our desires, wants and wishes.
– For Schopenhauer, our desires (wants, wishes, etc.) are the ultimate source of human suffering. They are at the heart of the illusion that it is possible to control what takes place in the

world. In fact, however, we have no control over whether or not our desires will be satisfied. In the face of this, the only ethically correct attitude to adopt and the only one that will make for a happy life, is that of abandoning or letting go of one's desires. We are free only to the extent that we can alter our attitude in this way. This restricted but fundamental freedom is made possible by the fact that we possess a noumenal will, as well as a phenomenal one.

iii. LOGICAL CLARITY AND THE FUNDAMENTAL CONTINGENCY OF THE WORLD

So now let us look at why exactly Wittgenstein takes issue with Schopenhauer's views on ethics, causality and determinism.

We know that Wittgenstein read Schopenhauer avidly and that he was much influenced by him. (In the *Notebooks*, he even went through a phase in which his thinking on ethics was, in many respects, close to Schopenhauer's.) But by the time he came to write the *Tractatus*, Wittgenstein had moved away from his earlier Schopenhauerian views and he had done so largely because his own views on logic had become clearer. This may seem puzzling. How can a change in one's views on logic be connected to a change in one's ethics? Indeed, what does logic even have to do with ethics? The answer in Wittgenstein's case is: everything. In fact he sees logic and ethics as being intimately intertwined: Wittgenstein's understanding of the logical nature of the world in the *Tractatus* is central to the book's unique and surprising ethical dimension.

Part of the aim of the *Tractatus*, then, is to offer a critique of Schopenhauer's ethics. The first and most obvious element of this critique targets Schopenhauer's conception of the world. According to Schopenhauer, the world is subject to causal necessity: everything in the world is the product of a long-standing, complex network of causes and effects – effects that are connected to their causes by means of necessary connections. It is for this reason that Schopenhauer holds that freedom cannot be located in the world. Human beings are unfree because everything in the world – including their phenomenal will (the desires, wants and wishes that motivate their actions) – is subject to causal necessity. This means in particular that any sense we may have of controlling the world, of being the ultimate source of what takes place in the world, is an illusion.

Interestingly, Wittgenstein also believes that this notion of control is an illusion. But his reasons for holding this view are diametrically opposite to Schopenhauer's.

According to Wittgenstein, Schopenhauer's conception of the world as subject to causal necessity is confused. Wittgenstein believes that his logical work, in the *Tractatus*, shows this to be the case. Part of the aim of the *Tractatus* is to clarify the concept of world. This process of conceptual clarification leads Wittgenstein to the conclusion that reality is the totality of facts – that is, the totality of obtaining states of affairs. Wittgenstein also concludes that states of affairs are radically independent from each other: states of affairs are, as he puts it, 'logically independent' from each other. The *Tractatus*' notion of logical independence is a little technical, so let us take a moment to consider it.

As we saw in Chapter 1, states of affairs are the most basic of possibilities: they are the possible states represented by the most basic of propositions, that is, by elementary propositions. Wittgenstein suggests that states of affairs are logically independent from each other in that the obtaining (or non-obtaining) of a one state of affairs cannot determine the obtaining (or non-obtaining) of another state of affairs. This can be put in terms of elementary propositions: elementary propositions are logically independent of each other in that that the truth-value of one elementary proposition cannot determine the truth-value of another elementary proposition; the truth (or falsity) of one elementary proposition can have no implications for the truth (of falsity) of another elementary proposition.

The idea that elementary propositions are logically independent from each other is crucial to the *Tractatus*. Its vital role is in reconciling two *Tractatus* ideas that are potentially at odds with each other: the idea that ordinary propositions result from applying logical operations to elementary propositions and the idea that all propositions are bipolar – that is, that they are both *capable* of being true and *capable* of being false.

As we saw in Chapter 1, the *Tractatus* suggests that, for something to be a genuine proposition, it needs to be genuinely informative about the world. This means that a proposition, if it is a genuine proposition, needs to be bipolar: it needs to be *both* capable of being true and capable of being false. At the same time, the *Tractatus* suggests that propositions result from applying logical operations to elementary propositions. It is these two ideas taken together that lead Wittgenstein to suggest that elementary propositions must be logically independent from each other. Why exactly does he feel the need to suggest this? His concern seems to have been that, if elementary propositions were logically *dependent* on each other, their combinations would not produce bipolar propositions. Imagine that 'a' and 'b' are logically dependent on each other, so that their truth-values are always the converse of each other: if 'a' is true, then 'b' is false; if 'a' is false then 'b' is true; and vice-versa. In that case, the conjunction of 'a' and 'b' – that is, 'a and b' – would be necessarily false. In this example, 'a and b' is not capable of being true; it is false in all circumstances. If 'a' is true, then 'b' is false, and then 'a and b' as a whole is false; in turn, if 'a' is false, then 'b' is true, and then 'a and b' as a whole remains false.

From this we can see why Wittgenstein believes that elementary propositions must be logically independent from each other: it is to guarantee that applying logical operations to them will produce bipolar propositions (i.e. propositions that are genuinely informative about the world). Without the condition that elementary propositions are logically independent, Wittgenstein would not be able to hold both that ordinary propositions are genuinely informative and that they result from applying logical operations to elementary propositions. The idea that ordinary propositions are ultimately analyzable into logically independent elementary propositions is therefore right at the heart of the *Tractatus*. For Wittgenstein, this is part and parcel of the very concept of proposition: propositions must be bipolar if they are to be informative; at the same time, they are the result of applying logical operations to elementary propositions consisting of names with simple meanings (since, as we saw in Chapter 1, this is a requirement of the determinacy of sense). These two requirements together entail that elementary propositions must be logically independent of each other. As a result, states of affairs (the senses of elementary propositions) must be logically independent of each other.

For Wittgenstein, the world (reality) is the totality of obtaining states of affairs. States of affairs are logically independent from each other: the obtaining (or non-obtaining) of one state of affairs cannot determine the obtaining (or non-obtaining) of another state of affairs. This entails, however, that there can be no necessary connections between obtaining states of affairs (between facts): the obtaining of one state of affairs cannot necessarily entail the obtaining (or, indeed, non-obtaining) of another state of affairs. One of the upshots of this, though, is that there is no causal necessity in the world, in Schopenhauer's sense: there are no relations of causal necessity between facts. If you remember, according to Schopenhauer, causation involves necessary connections between causes and effects: if A causes B, then, if A obtains, this entails that B also, *necessarily*, obtains; if A (the cause) obtains, it is logically impossible for B (the effect) not to obtain. But in Wittgenstein's view, this type of causal necessity is not in fact compatible with the notion of a state of affairs. States of affairs have to be logically independent from each other: the fact that one of them (e.g. A) obtains cannot entail that another one (e.g. B) obtains; nor can the obtaining of one (A) entail the non-obtaining of another (B). Wittgenstein argues that there are no necessary connections between states of affairs. As a result, Schopenhauer's conception of causation as involving necessity must be confused.

Wittgenstein devotes a good deal of very complex logical discussion to persuading us of this in the *Tractatus* – so much so, indeed, that it is rather too much for us to cover in any depth at this point. Instead, I am going to suggest that we focus on Wittgenstein's conclusion and take the process by which he gets there on trust for now. That conclusion is, in essence, that the states of affairs that make up the world are logically independent from each other; and that this quality of logical independence means that causal necessity, as Schopenhauer defines it, forms no part of the make-up of the world.

We have seen that Schopenhauer believes that human beings are powerless to affect what takes place in reality because the world is a strongly deterministic. Our desires and actions do not ultimately originate in us: we do not freely choose them, they are the product of causal chains that predate us, ones involving necessary connections between causes and effects, and this is what makes us powerless. Wittgenstein too believes that we are fundamentally powerless. However, his reasons for holding this are exactly the converse of Schopenhauer's. For Wittgenstein, our powerlessness comes from the fact that there is *no* causal necessity *whatsoever* in the world. The reason why we cannot control what takes place in the world is *not* that the world is governed by chains of causal necessity that predate us; the reason is that the world does not feature any causally necessary chains (in Schopenhauer's sense) at all.

This can be made clearer if we consider what would need to be the case in order to be able to say of someone that they genuinely control what takes place in the world. According to both Wittgenstein and Schopenhauer, I can only be said to have genuine control over my action of walking across the park if I am its ultimate source. And by 'ultimate source' what is meant, on this occasion, is ultimate *cause* – where 'cause' is understood as involving necessary connections. In this view, therefore, I can only be said to be genuinely in control of my action if:

(a) I am the ultimate cause of this action.
(b) There is a necessary connection between I (the cause) my action (the effects).

For Schopenhauer, (b) holds but (a) does not: my lack of control results from a failure to satisfy (a). For Wittgenstein, in contrast, my lack of control results primarily from a failure to satisfy (b). As we saw above, Wittgenstein believes that there is no causal necessity in the world: when one grasps the concept of world fully (this is the process that Wittgenstein covers at length in the *Tractatus*, and which we are currently taking on trust) one comes to see that the world features no causal necessity whatsoever. There are no necessary connections between causes and effects in the world. Causes and effects are not related in such a way that, if the cause obtains, it is impossible for the effect not to obtain. In particular, there are no necessary connections between my desires and the effects of my desires. Imagine that I genuinely desire to walk across the park: this is the only desire I have and it is a very strong one. Nevertheless, according to Wittgenstein, it is *possible* that I may end up not walking across the park, in spite of having this very strong desire. It is not just that I may be blown by a gale force wind in another direction, and may therefore be unable to satisfy my desire. The point is more subtle and – perhaps – more disturbing than that. For the idea is that, since there are no necessary connections whatsoever between my desires and my actions, I may have this very strong desire and nevertheless find that the desired action simply does not follow. This is a possibility, for Wittgenstein. In other words, it is *not* the case that: given A (the cause, my desire), it is impossible that B (the effect, my walking across the park) should not obtain. For Wittgenstein, we are fundamentally powerless not because the world is subject to strong causal determination that has us in its grip, but because it features no causal necessity that would allow our desires to necessarily entail consequences. This means, in particular, that there is no necessary connection between my desiring something and my desire being satisfied: I may have an irrepressible, single-minded desire to walk across the park, but there is no genuine guarantee that my desire will be satisfied. Indeed, it may well not be.

According to Wittgenstein, our fundamental powerlessness comes not from the fact that the world is strongly causal, but from the very opposite: it arises from the total absence of causal necessity in the world. There are no necessary causal connections between facts in the world, not even at the most basic level. So there is, for instance, no necessary connection between my desire to move my hand (i.e. that particular mental fact) and the movement of my hand (that particular physical fact). Whether or not my hand ends up moving is an entirely *contingent* matter. 'Contingent' here means that the movement of my hand is a possibility, but that this possibility is not *necessarily connected* to the initial desire to move it – nor indeed to any other fact that happens to obtain. The fact that I desire something does not *necessarily* bring it about. Wittgenstein therefore agrees with Schopenhauer in saying that we are fundamentally unfree in this respect but differs in his understanding of why. As we will see in the next section, Wittgenstein's position also differs from Schopenhauer's in another crucial respect – one that sets Wittgenstein's ethics fundamentally apart from Schopenhauer's.

In Summary

– Wittgenstein's work on logic and representation in the *Tractatus* leads him to the conclusion that, far from being strongly deterministic, the world is fundamentally contingent. In particular, the world is not subject to causal necessity: facts are not connected to each other by relations of causal necessity.

– Wittgenstein agrees with Schopenhauer's view that we are fundamentally powerless. He disagrees with Schopenhauer as to the reason for this, however. For Wittgenstein, we are fundamentally powerless because causal necessity is an illusion – in particular, there are no necessary connections between my desires and the facts that would satisfy them. Whether or not my desires are satisfied is a purely contingent matter: it is possible that they will, but it is just as possible that they won't. I exert no genuine influence over the world, on the basis of my desires.

iv. THE ETHICAL POINT OF THE *TRACTATUS*

Wittgenstein insists that the point of the *Tractatus* is an ethical point. As we saw at the beginning of this chapter, this claim is in many respects surprising. After all, the *Tractatus* includes very few remarks that could be regarded as touching on ethical themes. Of these remarks, many appear to be negative, being as they are primarily concerned with what ethics is *not*, rather than with what ethics *is*. Why then is ethics so central to the *Tractatus*, in Wittgenstein's view? As we will now see, the answer to this question has to do with Wittgenstein's very particular view of ethics.

For Wittgenstein, the world is fundamentally contingent. There are no necessary causal connections between states of affairs. The obtaining of one state of affairs in no way guarantees the obtaining of another state of affairs; nor does it guarantee its non-obtaining. This logical view of the world has, for Wittgenstein, strong ethical implications. As we saw in the previous section, it entails that human beings are not genuinely in control of anything that takes place in the world. I am not even genuinely in control of my actions: my desire to walk across the park is in no way guaranteed to bring about the desired effect (the action of my walking across the park). According to Wittgenstein, this realization leads to a profound ethical transformation in one's outlook on the world. Imagine that I have a strong, overriding desire to move my hand and that my desire is satisfied: my hand does move. My hand could just as well not have moved; there is, in this respect, no necessary causal connection between my desire and the moving of my hand. It is possible that I might have a powerful desire to move my hand and that my hand might nevertheless fail to move. Then again, it is also possible that my hand might move. The obtaining of one fact (here the mental fact of my desire) does not *guarantee* that another fact (the moving of my hand) will obtain; nor does it guarantee that the other fact will fail to obtain (that my hand will fail to move). There are no necessary causal connections between facts in the world: no fact can necessarily cause another to obtain – or indeed to fail to obtain.

The question is, of course: why, exactly, is this related to ethics, for Wittgenstein? This becomes clearer when one considers how one comes to regard the obtaining of any fact, when one sees the world in this way. Imagine again that I have a strong desire to move my hand and that my hand does indeed move. In other words, imagine that the fact that satisfies my desire does indeed obtain. The moving of my hand (that fact) is something that need not have happened. There was no necessity to it happening. More specifically, there was no necessary connection between my desire to move my hand and my hand moving: my desire did not bring about, as a matter of causal necessity, the movement of my hand. And, yet, there goes my hand – moving: there goes the only fact that could satisfy my desire. Wittgenstein suggests that, as soon as one becomes clear that the world is fundamentally contingent, everything that happens in the world – including, here, the movement of my hand – starts to look like a gift of fate. Every fact starts to look like something quite extraordinary and, given that it could not have obtained, quite fragile. That any facts whatsoever should obtain, given that they *need not*, is, for this reason, of profound ethical value, in Wittgenstein's view.

This is quite a subtle and complex idea, so let us consider it again. It starts with the idea that everything that takes place in the world could, just as conceivably, not have obtained. Everything in the world is fragile, in the sense of being fundamentally contingent: all of the facts that make up reality are such that they could possibly not have obtained – their obtaining was not guaranteed by the obtaining of any prior facts. When one views the world in this way, it becomes a source of intense wonder that there should be anything – that there should be this reality – *at all*. For it becomes clear that the world is fundamentally fragile – this reality could, at any point, cease to exist; furthermore, it could, simply, never have existed. This sense of the fundamental contingency of the world is, in Wittgenstein's view, the source of all ethical value. Once one realizes that everything is fragile in this way, one comes to regard everything – every fact – in the world as an extraordinary gift – as something profoundly valuable.

One possible question that might emerge at this point is: does Wittgenstein accept that there might be some other type of connection between causes and effects – say a relation of probability, rather than one of necessity? In other words, would Wittgenstein be happy with the idea that my desire to move my hand makes the movement of my hand more likely (more probable), even if it does not guarantee it (even if no necessary connection holds between the two)? There is much debate on Wittgenstein's views on probability – so much so that unfortunately it is impossible to consider this question in any detail here. Whatever Wittgenstein may have thought on this subject, however, it seems clear that for him it is the lack of a necessary connection between causes and effects that is central to ethics. His view seems to have been that, even if it could be established that my desire makes the moving of my hand more likely, still, because it does not guarantee it, the movement of my hands must ultimately be regarded as outside my control: it must ultimately be regarded a gift from fate. Viewed in this way, the movement of my hand (and, indeed, my desire to move my hand) remain profoundly valuable. But Wittgenstein claims that the *Tractatus'* ultimate point is an ethical one. Why should the movement of my hand have any ethical significance? In particular, what exactly would it have to do with the notion of ethical value or ethical good? The *Tractatus* is silent on this matter. The reasons for this silence are complicated; they are to do with the idea we mentioned earlier in this chapter: the idea that ethics cannot be put into words. This is something we will be returning to below. Before we turn to this issue, I would like to consider in a little more detail the relation that exists for Wittgenstein between the contingency of the world and its ethical value.

In order to throw light on this relation, it is useful to consider a text that Wittgenstein wrote years after completing the *Tractatus*: his 'Lecture on Ethics', which he presented in 1929 at the meeting of a Cambridge society. At this time, although his views were evolving, Wittgenstein continued to uphold the ethical insights that had emerged from the *Tractatus* – arguably, he held them for the rest of his life – as well as the idea that ethics is essentially indescribable in language. At the same time, he had abandoned enough of his earlier views on language to feel able to discuss the subject in a little further detail than he had in the *Tractatus*.

In his 'Lecture on Ethics', Wittgenstein introduces an important distinction – a distinction that throws light on his entire approach to ethics: the distinction between 'relative' and 'absolute' value. According to Wittgenstein, we value facts *relatively* when we only value them in so far as are useful to us. More specifically, something is of relative value to me when it is a *means* by which I can satisfy some desire. In other words, things have relative value when their value derives from the fact that they can be used as a means to achieve an end that we desire. Imagine, for instance, that I view my fountain pen exclusively as a means to my end of writing: imagine that I view it exclusively as a means to satisfy my desire to write. In that case, the pen only has relative value for me: it is valuable to me only in so far as it is useful to me, only in so far as it is a means to satisfy my desire for writing.

It is really important to notice the connection between this notion of relative value and what, for Wittgenstein, is a mistaken, illusory conception of the world: the conception that suggests that we are – at least to some extent – in control of what happens in the world. For to value something relatively is to value it in so far as it is an *effective means to satisfy some desire*. But one only views things in this way when one is prey to the illusion of control. To put is differently: once I become clear as to the fundamental contingency of the world – once I realize that there is nothing I can do to *guarantee* that my desires will be satisfied – the very idea of searching for the *means* to satisfy my desires loses its grip. The fountain pen is simply not an 'effective means' to satisfy my desire to write, since there is no guarantee that it will satisfy that desire. Once I become clear that I cannot bring about (as a matter of causal necessity) anything in the world, the very idea of trying to secure the *means* to my ends loses all significance. If the world is fundamentally contingent, if there is no causal necessity at work in the world, then the very notion of there being means to certain ends falls apart – and with it, the notion that certain things possess relative value.

So essentially Wittgenstein introduces the notion of 'relative value' in order to discredit it and demonstrate that it is fundamentally flawed. The temptation to place relative value on things vanishes as soon as one becomes clear that the world is fundamentally contingent. As soon as it becomes clear that causal necessity is an illusion this notion of valuing loses all of its attraction. In its place, Wittgenstein suggests, a different way of valuing starts to emerge. Faced with the fundamental contingency of the world, we come to value the world in an *absolute* – rather than relative – manner. In his 'Lecture on Ethics', Wittgenstein explains that he associates the notion of absolute value with the experience of '[wondering] at the existence of the world', that is, with the experience that makes him inclined 'to use such phrases as "how extraordinary that anything should exist" or "how extraordinary that the world should exist"' (p. 8). The world (the totality of facts) is fundamentally contingent: it need not have been, it could, just as conceivably, not have existed. There was nothing to guarantee that it would come into existence; and nothing guarantees that it will continue to exist in the future. In the absence of causal necessity, there are simply no guarantees with respect to what facts obtain or will continue to obtain in the future. As soon as we come to realize this, we start valuing the world in an absolute manner. The entire world (the whole of reality) becomes imbued with a sense of wonder for us: that there should be anything at all, given that everything could not have existed, is extraordinary. When viewed in this way, everything acquires an absolute sense of worth.

For Wittgenstein, then, it is (or should be!) a source of profound wonder that *any* possible state should obtain as a fact. This sense of wonder arises in connection to *all* facts: physical facts (the rocks, plants, animals, human physical bodies we encounter in reality) and mental facts. As we saw in the last chapter, mental facts include desires, beliefs, wishes, and, more broadly, minds. This is important, because it marks a crucial difference between Wittgenstein's ethics and Schopenhauer's. In Wittgenstein's view, the process of conceptual clarification of the *Tractatus* culminates in the realization that desires are mental facts and that all facts are fundamentally contingent. Becoming clear about this is coming to view our desires (along with all other facts) with a profound sense of wonder. That I should have any desires – that these mental facts should obtain at all – is quite extraordinary. As soon as one starts to view one's desires in this way, one comes to value them absolutely, as a precious and fragile gift. This, of course, differs in an important way from Schopenhauer's view on desire. As we saw earlier, Schopenhauer believes that we can and should *choose* the attitude of *abandoning* our desires. I cannot freely choose what desires I have, but I can choose to let go of those desires. Imagine that I have a desire for warmth. I cannot choose to have a desire for coldness instead, but I can let go of my desire for warmth: I can choose to abandon my desire for warmth. To this limited extent, freedom is possible within Schopenhauer's view: I am free to choose to let go of those desires I do have. Letting go of my desires is the ethically correct choice, for Schopenhauer: my life will be a good, happy life if I make this choice.

Wittgenstein's position is different. To begin with, there is in his view no suggestion that we are faced with an ethical *choice*. He allows that there are two possible attitudes towards the world, but he does not suggest that we *choose* (let alone *freely* choose) between them. Instead, Wittgenstein's suggestion is that our attitude towards the world goes hand in hand with the conception of the world we happen to have. I do not freely choose between valuing things relatively or valuing them absolutely, just as I do not freely choose between the confused and the enlightened conceptions of the world. Rather, I am confused about the world and value things in a relative manner, or I have a clear conception of the world in which I value the world absolutely – I cannot voluntarily switch from one to the other.

The confused conception of the world involves the illusion that there are relations of causal necessity in the world, that we are, as a matter of causal necessity, in control of some of the facts. The attitude of valuing facts *relatively* – the attitude of valuing facts as means towards our desired ends – is part of this confused conception of the world. Being aware of the fundamental contingency of the world, in contrast, involves viewing the world with a profound sense of wonder: it involves valuing it *absolutely* it as an extraordinary gift. There is no choice to be made between the two attitudes: it is not as if I can choose between two attitudes that are equally available to me at any one point. Instead I find that, at any given point in time, I either conceive the world clearly and value it absolutely (in which case I am not conceptually confused and do not value the world relatively) or I value facts in a relative manner as part of a confused conception of the world (in which case I do not, at that time, have a clear conception of the world and do not value facts absolutely).

Wittgenstein's view therefore differs from Schopenhauer's with respect to the issue of choice: for Schopenhauer, there is a free choice to be made, albeit a limited one; for Wittgenstein, there simply isn't. Wittgenstein's view also differs from Schopenhauer's in another important respect: it differs in its treatment of desire. Both philosophers agree that we cannot change our desires: I cannot choose to have a desire for coldness rather than a desire for warmth. However, they differ in their treatments of the desires we do have. Schopenhauer recommends that we strive to *abandon* or let go of the desires we do have: I should, in this example, try to let go of my desire for warmth. For Wittgenstein, in contrast, my desire for warmth is part of the fundamentally contingent reality (of the world as totality of facts). As such, it is a source of profound wonder and it is to be valued, in and of itself, in an absolute manner. Instead of attempting to let go of the desires we do have, we should simply value them for the fundamentally fragile gifts they are. Valuing them in this way involves, of course, recognizing that attempting to fulfil them may prove to be an inherently pointless endeavour.

Before we draw this chapter to a close, it is worth sounding a note of caution. For Wittgenstein's position could be understood as an invitation to cease all action or as an invitation to stop striving towards anything. If I am not genuinely in control of anything, what is the point in my attempting to act? And what is the point in my trying to improve myself in any way? This is not at all Wittgenstein's position however. Indeed, we should note that this suggestion (the suggestion that one should cease trying to act or strive towards anything) relies on the notion that I *am*, in fact, in control of at least some aspects of my life: I am sufficiently in control to make the decision to cease to act or to cease to strive! Wittgenstein sees this as a misapprehension. I may, at any given time, have the *desire* to stop acting or the desire to stop improving myself, but there is absolutely no guarantee that these desires will be satisfied: I may have these desires and yet continue to act and continue to try to improve myself.

For Wittgenstein, the key really is in our recognizing the fundamental contingency of all facts presented before us: whether these facts are desires to continue improving ourselves or desires to give up, whether they are actions or inactions. While Wittgenstein was developing the *Tractatus*, the notion of trying to improve himself – of desiring to become a better (i.e. a clearer and more authentic) person – was central to him, and would remain so for the rest of his life. After all, his ethics crystallized while he was fighting in World War I, on the Austro-Hungarian side. Wittgenstein's attitude during the war is very telling of his ethics. Not only did he join the war as a volunteer, but he then strove not to be left behind the lines but to be posted to the front, where the real danger lay. When his desire to go to the front was finally granted by the military authorities (almost two years later!), he continued applying for the most dangerous tasks. He seems to have regarded the experience of putting his life at risk as a crucial test of character, one that would help him in his struggle to become a better person.[9] Crucially, in his view there was no inconsistency between the desire to improve himself (the desire for whatever actions might bring this improvement) and the recognition that this desire might never be granted.

In Summary

- For Wittgenstein, being clear as to the fundamental contingency of the world involves valuing the world as a whole in an absolute manner. In contrast, conceiving the world confusedly as subject to causal necessity involves valuing facts in a relative manner.
- Wittgenstein's ethics does not involve making free choices. There is no choice to be made between the attitude of relative valuing and that of absolute valuing: it is not as if, at any one point, I can choose between two attitudes that are equally available to me.

v. CONCLUSION

So for Wittgenstein, the point of the *Tractatus* is an ethical one. This is not to say that the book describes or presents an ethical theory, however. Indeed, according to Wittgenstein, ethical value cannot be put into words: it cannot be described in language. The reason for this has to do with Wittgenstein's conception of language. As we saw in Chapter 1, language describes possible ways in which reality might be: propositions represent possible states. Ethical value is not a possible state, however; instead, valuing consists in adopting a certain attitude towards the possible states that obtain as facts in reality. Since propositions only describe possible states and since ethical value is not a possible state, ethical value cannot be described by means of propositions: it cannot be described by presenting ethical theories inevitably couched in language. The very few remarks of the *Tractatus* that touch upon the ethical do not attempt to put forward an ethical theory. Indeed, these remarks are, for the most part, negative in tone: they concern what ethics is *not*, rather than what ethics *is*. They are part of a critique of traditional ethical theories, but this critique does not involve putting forward alternative theories.

Instead, the point of the *Tractatus* is an ethical one in that the book offers us the possibility of engaging in a process of conceptual clarification. If we happen to engage in this process and if the process is successful, we will gain a clearer conception of the world and will come to value it in an absolute manner. The point of the *Tractatus* is an ethical one, therefore, in that it opens up for us the possibility of a profound ethical transformation.

Wittgenstein's approach to ethics is subtle and, frankly, difficult. Part of the reason for this difficulty is that his approach runs counter the three central tenets of the traditional conception of ethics: the idea that ethics can be described in language; the idea that motive and action are central to ethics; and the idea that freedom is a prerequisite of ethics. (Since this traditional conception has done much to shape our common-sense ethical intuitions – our notions of right and wrong, of human justice, and so forth – it is no wonder that an approach that runs against it should prove difficult to assimilate.) In Wittgenstein's view, ethics cannot be described by means of propositions: value is not a possible state and, since language can only represent possible states, language cannot represent value. Secondly, ethics is not primarily to do with motives and actions. Ethics, for Wittgenstein, consists in having a clear sense of the fundamental contingency of world and in valuing the world as a whole – the world as the totality of facts – in an absolute manner. Our motives (our desires, our beliefs, etc.) and our actions are facts among many others. They have no special significance, from this point of view: they do not stand out as being (ethically) more important than other facts. Our desires, our beliefs, our actions are perfectly on a par with other facts: from the point of view of what is important in ethics, they are on a par with facts concerning mountains or lakes or goats or lampposts. For Wittgenstein, all facts are fundamentally contingent: all facts are, for this reason, exactly on the same level. The ethical attitude consists in recognizing the fundamental contingency of all facts and in valuing them absolutely as awe-inspiring, precious gifts. Finally, Wittgenstein's ethics runs counter to the traditional idea that freedom is a prerequisite of ethics. In Wittgenstein's view, there are no free choices to be made in this area.

CONCLUSION TO PART I

So far we have seen that, for Wittgenstein, the task of philosophy is that of clarifying concepts. The process of conceptual clarification that the *Tractatus* engages us in is important for two main reasons: first, because conceptual confusion is at the root of the most intractable problems in philosophy, problems such as that of solipsism, which we discussed in Chapter 2; secondly because, as we saw in Chapter 3, conceptual clarity has a fundamental ethical dimension, since being clear about the contingency of the world involves valuing the world in an absolute (rather than relative) manner.

In the *Tractatus*, Wittgenstein works at clarifying a series of concepts, among them the concepts of sentence, of proposition, of world, of picture, of thought and of self. As we saw in Chapter 1, Wittgenstein indicates that a sentence is an arrangement of words that can be used to represent a variety of possible states, a variety of possibilities. When a sentence is used to represent one particular possible state (one particular possible way in which reality might be) it becomes (or expresses) a proposition with a sense. He suggests that propositions are central to the communication of thought. I can communicate my thought to you by presenting you with a proposition that represents the same possible state represented by my thought. Propositions and thoughts are both strictly logical pictures for Wittgenstein – an idea we examined in Chapter 2.

The view that philosophy aims at the clarification of concepts means that certain questions can only be taken so far, when they are asked from the philosophical perspective. Consider, for instance, the question: how do we recognize whether a sentence expresses one proposition rather than another? Wittgenstein answers this question by gesturing towards the notion of how a sentence is used:

In order to recognise a [proposition] by its [sentence, its propositional sign] we must observe how it is *used* with a sense. (TLP 3.326, my italics)

We *use* the perceptible sign of a proposition (spoken or written, etc.) as a projection of a possible situation. (TLP 3.1, my italics)

Still, we may ask, what *is it* to recognize how the sentence is used? This question can be understood in (at least) two different ways. First, it can be understood as a philosophical question – that is as a question asking for a clarification as to what is *essential* to the concepts of sentence and of proposition. When the question is understood in this way, however, we cannot get very far in answering it. Wittgenstein suggests that from the perspective of philosophy (from the perspective of the clarification of concepts) all we can do is note that recognizing how a sentence is used involves exercising an *ability* (namely, the ability to recognise how sentences are used). The question 'what is it to recognize how the sentence is used?' can only be taken this far if it is understood as a philosophical question (i.e. one concerned with the clarification of concepts).

This question can, however, be pushed further if it is understood in a different way. That is, it can be pushed further if it is understood as a question for the natural sciences, as a question asked from the perspective of trying to establish the *facts* of the matter. Understood in this way, the question is really asking what, in reality, happens to be the *mechanism* that enables us to recognize how a sentence is used (what proposition it expresses). The question, understood in this way, is of course an important one – but, crucially for Wittgenstein, it is not a question for *philosophy*. It needs instead to be answered by those who investigate the facts of the matter about language: by psychologists, neurologists, physiologists, etc. From the point of view of philosophy, the question understood in this way is not relevant because it is not asking what is *essential* to the concepts under examination. It may be that, in reality, a series of electrochemical exchanges in the brain are involved in language recognition. But it is also *conceivable* that they should not have been so involved. That is: it is possible (in the sense of conceivable, imaginable) that, if our physiology had been different, the mechanism involved in language recognition might too have been different. In this respect, it is possible that we might one day be able to communicate in language with creatures whose physiology is very different from us. Identifying factual mechanisms is different from clarifying what is essential to concepts. The conceptual nature of the philosopher's task means that questions must be interpreted in particular ways and that they can only go so far. If we try to push them further, we end up generating confused pseudo-concepts that give rise to apparently intractable philosophical problems. This is something we discussed in Chapter 2, when we examined Russell's notion of the simple thinking self and its connection to solipsism.

Philosophy is the task of clarifying concepts – concepts such as that of proposition, sentence, thought, world, etc. And, in the *Tractatus*, Wittgenstein believes himself to have pushed this process of conceptual clarification as far as it will happily go. This gives rise to an important question, however. The question is: how, exactly, does the *Tractatus* go about clarifying these concepts? How does it succeed in conveying this conceptual clarity to us?

One possible answer here would be: the *Tractatus* succeeds in clarifying these concepts by presenting us with senseful propositions. If we were to take this view we would be saying that the *Tractatus* is made up of senseful propositions and that it is through these senseful propositions that it goes about its task of conceptual clarification. There is a serious problem with this view, however. For, by the *Tractatus*' own lights, a proposition is a sentence that represents a *possible state* – that is, as we saw in Chapter 1, something that is both *capable* of obtaining and *capable* of failing to obtain. Clarifying concepts is not about affirming possibilities, however: the clarificatory expression 'a bachelor is an unmarried man' does not represent something that is merely possible, it does not represent something that is both capable of obtaining and capable of failing to obtain. Given the concept of bachelor, it is a matter of *conceptual necessity* that a bachelor should be a unmarried man.[10] In this respect, therefore 'a bachelor is an unmarried man' is not capable of being false at all: it does not represent something capable of failing to obtain. If we follow this logic through, we can see that the clarificatory sentence 'a bachelor is an unmarried man' is not a senseful proposition. The purpose of the expression 'a bachelor is an unmarried man' is not to represent a possible state, but to give us an instruction: an instruction as to how to use the word 'bachelor'. (The instruction here would be roughly as follows: use 'bachelor' as a substitute for 'unmarried man'.)

The sentences of the *Tractatus* (certainly most of them) are not senseful propositions either. Consider, for example, the three primary remarks of the book (primary in the sense of being the first in their number series):

The world is all that is the case. (TLP 1)

What is the case – a fact – is the existence of states of affairs. (TLP 2)

A logical picture of facts is a thought. (TLP 3)

These remarks are clearly (at least in some respects) reminiscent of 'a bachelor is an unmarried man'. They are clarificatory expressions or – as Wittgenstein sometimes calls them – 'elucidations'. They are used, not to describe possibilities, but to do something else: to give us instructions, to instruct us as to the use of certain. If Wittgenstein did regard the *Tractatus* as fulfilling the aim of clarifying concepts, then it is possible – indeed it is likely – that he regarded the sentences of the *Tractatus* as clarificatory (or elucidatory) instructions. The sentences of the *Tractatus* are not used to describe possibilities, but to direct us, to give us guidance, in our *activity* of using of signs. They are not propositions with senses, in Wittgenstein's own understanding of the term, but 'elucidations':

Philosophy aims at the logical clarification of thoughts.
Philosophy is not a body of doctrine but an *activity*.
A philosophical work consists essentially of elucidations.
Philosophy does not result in 'philosophical propositions', but rather in the *clarification* of propositions. (TLP 4.112, my italics)

The question of the status of the expressions that make up the *Tractatus* is, in fact, even more complex than I have made it sound. Part of the reason for this complexity is that many of the concepts elucidated in the *Tractatus* are different from the concept of bachelor: they are what Wittgenstein calls 'formal concepts' – a notion that for reasons of space we will not be examining here.

Nevertheless, I think it is fair to say that many of the expressions that make up the *Tractatus* are intended as instructions: they purport to instruct us in the use of certain signs. In this respect, part of the aim of the *Tractatus* is to help us refine our *abilities* or our skills in the use of signs. Refining our abilities in this way involves coming to treat propositions as possessing determinate senses and therefore as being ultimately analyzable into elementary propositions consisting of names with simple meanings, etc. This approach to propositions is predicated on the idea that there is an important distinction between what propositions *say* (the possibilities they represent) and what they *show*. How signs are used in propositions is shown, not said, by propositions.

What signs fail to express, their application shows. (TLP 3.262)

Furthermore, Wittgenstein adds that:

What *can* be shown, *cannot* be said. (TLP 4.1212)

The *Tractatus* aims at clarifying the concept of senseful proposition, among others. Clarifying this concept involves clarifying how signs are used in propositions. Since this cannot be *said*, however, it is not surprising that Wittgenstein should have regarded the remarks that make up the *Tractatus*, not as senseful propositions that say (or represent) possible states, but as elucidations or instructions lacking in sense. The notion of what cannot be said but that nevertheless shows itself is central both to Wittgenstein's approach to the proposition and to his views on other areas, such as that of ethics. In this respect, it is not surprising that Wittgenstein should have chosen to end the *Tractatus* with the remark:

What we cannot speak about we must pass over in silence. (TLP 7)

PART II

THE LATER WITTGENSTEIN

CHAPTER 4

LANGUAGE AND USE

i. INTRODUCTION

By the time the *Tractatus* was finally published in 1921, Wittgenstein believed that he had solved all of the problems of philosophy. Under these circumstances, what was a philosopher to do? For Wittgenstein, the answer was perfectly obvious. In a coherent though somewhat radical move, he took the eminently logical step of abandoning his philosophical work entirely and returning to his native Austria to start a new life. Upon returning to Austria, he gave away his part of the family inheritance and went on to spend several years applying himself with mixed success to a variety of professions: he was a gardener, a primary school teacher and an architect, among others. His attempt to cut himself off from philosophy was not wholly successful, however. In 1927, after an initial reluctance, he accepted an invitation to take part in the philosophical discussions of the 'Vienna Circle', a group of philosophers led by Morris Schlick. Through these meetings he began thinking about philosophy again, a process that eventually led him to resume his philosophical work in earnest. When he finally returned to Cambridge, in 1929, his thoughts – though still very much dominated by the *Tractatus* – were already starting to change. In the years that followed, he would reject many of his earlier views on language, thought and logic. In so doing, he would come to pioneer a new, once again revolutionary approach to philosophy.

In this chapter, we will introduce Wittgenstein's new approach to philosophy and see how it contrasts with the *Tractatus*'. We will do this by focusing primarily on Wittgenstein's discussion of language, in the *Philosophical Investigations*. This will then put us in a position to examine Wittgenstein's later treatment of rules and of sensations, in Chapters 5 and 6 respectively.

ii. THE DEMISE OF THE *TRACTATUS*

One way to describe the shift from Wittgenstein's earlier to later philosophies is to say that Wittgenstein's aims remain the same but that the method he employs in trying to achieve these aims is radically different. In both periods, Wittgenstein sees his aim that of clarifying concepts. For Wittgenstein, the task of the philosopher remains one of conceptual clarification – this idea stays central to Wittgenstein's thinking throughout his life. However, his understanding of the nature of concepts and, with it, his understanding of what is involved in clarifying them, undergoes a complete transformation in his later philosophical period.

As we saw in earlier chapters, Wittgenstein sees himself, in the *Tractatus*, as engaged in a task of conceptual clarification. This task is important because traditional philosophy is plagued with problems that result from confusions in our concepts – problems that can only be resolved by clarifying the concepts in question. In the *Tractatus*, Wittgenstein has a very particular view of what is involved in clarifying a concept. In this view, concepts have a fixed, clearly demarcated set of essential features – to clarify a concept is therefore to emphasize the essential features (the 'essence') of this concept and to distinguish these essential features from the concept's inessential or accidental features. For example, Wittgenstein suggests, in the *Tractatus*, that it is essential for propositions to have a determinate truth-value (to be determinately either true or false) and that it is essential for them to be logically analyzable into elementary arrangements of names with simple meanings. In contrast, it is *not* essential for a proposition to be expressed by means of English-language (or Spanish-language) signs. Possessing a determinate truth-value and being logically analyzable into elementary propositions are essential features of propositions to the extent that without them, propositions would simply not be propositions at all, according to the *Tractatus*. In contrast, something can be a proposition without being expressed in English (or indeed in Spanish). In Wittgenstein's earlier view, clarifying the concept of proposition involves uncovering the *essence* – the fixed, precise set of essential features – shared by all propositions. As we will see shortly, this view comes under attack in the *Philosophical Investigations*.

The second aspect of the *Tractatus* to come under attack in the *Philosophical Investigations* is the emphasis it places on the notion of logical analysis. As we saw before, the *Tractatus* views logical analysis as a key philosophical tool for the clarification of concepts. In what sense does logical analysis help with the clarification of concepts? The idea, as you may remember, is as follows. Imagine that John is not sure about the concept of '*bachelor*'. In other words, imagine that he is unsure as to what we mean when we talk of '*bachelors*'. If so, I could help clarify this concept for him by giving him the beginning of the logical analysis of '*bachelor*', for instance, by saying: 'bachelors are men' and 'bachelors are unmarried'. If John finds that he needs further clarifications, I can push this analysis further: I can say, for instance, 'bachelors are human beings' and 'bachelors are male' and NOT – 'bachelors are married', etc. In principle, I could, if necessary, push this logical analysis all the way to the level of elementary propositions, thereby revealing all of the essential features and the very precise internal structure of the concept of '*bachelor*'.

The *Tractatus*' view that concepts have fixed, precise essences and the view that logical analysis is central to the clarification of concepts are, of course, interconnected: logical analysis is a very precise, almost surgical tool; it is therefore particularly well suited to dissecting precise, clearly delimited concepts. However, both the view that concepts have fixed essences and the view that logical analysis is central to conceptual clarification are rejected by Wittgenstein in his later philosophical period. This rejection eventually leads him to an entirely new understanding of what is involved in clarifying concepts and, therefore, to an entirely new understanding of the task of the philosopher. What, we may ask, sets these changes in motion? Why does Wittgenstein come to reject the view that concepts have essences and the view that logical analysis is central to conceptual clarification? The answer to these questions lies in Wittgenstein's growing dissatisfaction with his *Tractatus* discussion of language.

As we saw in earlier chapters, Wittgenstein suggests in the *Tractatus* that all propositions share a set of essential features. All propositions represent possible states: they make statements about possible ways in which reality might be. All propositions are determinately true or false (they are bivalent). All propositions are both capable of being true and capable of being false (they are bipolar). All propositions result from applying logical operations to elementary propositions; indeed, all propositions are, in principle, logically analyzable into the elementary propositions that make them up. All propositions have a determinate sense; for this reason, the elementary propositions that make them up must consist of names with simple meanings. As we saw in Chapter 1, the latter two ideas are interconnected: there is, in Wittgenstein's view, an intimate connection between simplicity of meaning and determinacy of sense.

By the time Wittgenstein returned to Cambridge in 1929, he was becoming unhappy with this train of thought. One of the first problems he hit had to do with his earlier notion of logical independence. As we saw in Chapter 3, Wittgenstein holds, in the *Tractatus*, that elementary propositions – the purely logical propositions that emerge once ordinary propositions are completely analyzed – are logically independent from each other. This means that the truth-value of one elementary proposition cannot determine the truth-value of another: the truth (or falsity) of one elementary proposition can have no implications for the truth (of falsity) of another elementary proposition.

The idea that elementary propositions are logically independent from each other is crucial to the *Tractatus*. Its vital role is in reconciling two *Tractatus* ideas that are potentially at odds with each other: the idea that ordinary propositions result from applying logical operations to elementary propositions and the idea that all propositions are bipolar (i.e. that they are both *capable* of being true and *capable* of being false). As we saw in Chapter 1, the *Tractatus* suggests that sense would not be determinate if propositions did not result from applying logical operations to elementary propositions consisting of names with simple meanings; at the same time, propositions need to be bipolar, in this view, if they are to be informative about the world. In Chapter 3 we saw that these two ideas, together, lead to the idea that elementary propositions must be logically independent from each other: elementary propositions must be logically independent from each other so as to guarantee that applying logical operations to them will produce bipolar, informative propositions. The idea that ordinary propositions are ultimately analyzable into logically independent elementary propositions is therefore right at the heart of the *Tractatus*.

In 1929, though, Wittgenstein comes to realize that there are some serious problems with this idea. In fact, the idea turns out to be so problematic that it ends up bringing down the entire conceptual edifice of the *Tractatus*.

The issue that puts Wittgenstein on the path to abandoning the *Tractatus* is not, in fact, new to him. He is already aware of it when he writes the *Tractatus*; indeed, he mentions it in TLP 6.3751. It is just that, when he's writing the *Tractatus*, he thinks that the problem can easily be explained away. The problem is this: some of our ordinary propositions are clearly logically *dependent* on each other they are dependent on each other because of the way in which their concepts work; how can such propositions be the result of applying logical operations to logically *independent* propositions? As examples of ordinary, logically dependent propositions, consider, for instance, the propositions: 'this ball is blue all over at time t' and 'this ball is red all over at time t' – where 'this ball' picks out the same particular ball and 't' picks out the same particular time and date. These two propositions are logically dependent on each other: if 'this ball is blue all over at time t' is true, then 'this ball is red all over at time t' is false. The question is: how can such propositions be clearly logically dependent on each other if they are the result of applying operations to logically *independent* elementary propositions?

This is sometimes called the 'colour exclusion problem' because it involves the idea that propositions about colour exclude one another: colour concepts are such that one and the same thing cannot be genuinely blue and red all over at the same time. Although colour seems to have been the issue that triggered Wittgenstein's realization that his *Tractatus* argument was in trouble, the problem is not limited to propositions about colour. In fact, *any* proposition that expresses concepts that exclude one another in this way is affected by it. Consider, for instance, '*This line is one metre long*': if this proposition is true, then, necessarily, '*This line is three metres long*' is false. Ordinary propositions are very often logically dependent on each other in this way. Some commentators have even argued that the vast majority of – if not all – ordinary propositions are logically dependent on each other in some way.

The question, for Wittgenstein, is therefore: if elementary propositions are genuinely logically independent, how can they produce ordinary propositions that are not? Or, to put it differently: how can a non-independent ordinary proposition result from combining elementary propositions that are logically independent? When Wittgenstein writes the *Tractatus*, he is convinced that the colour exclusion problem poses no genuine threat to his view that elementary propositions are logically independent of each other. He believes that, if one carried out the complete analysis of propositions such as '*This ball is blue all over at time t*', their analysis would remove the apparent difficulty: logical analysis would show that these propositions do indeed break down into logically independent elementary propositions. But since Wittgenstein was the first to admit that he had never carried out such an analysis, he had no evidence to show that the problem was indeed solved. In the *Tractatus*, he had been, as it were, taking his own logical process on trust.

One of the first things that Wittgenstein does, when he returns to philosophy in 1929, is to think anew about this logical process of analysis and to consider how exactly it would unfold in practice. Very quickly – to his dismay – he comes to realize that in fact it cannot be made to work. The reasons for this are complex and we will not be examining them here in any detail.[11] What is crucial is that this realization starts a process that eventually leads him to abandon the very notion of logical independence. Since this notion is so central to the *Tractatus*, however, once it is discarded, the entire conceptual edifice starts toppling down. If elementary propositions are *not* logically independent, the idea that ordinary propositions are ultimately analyzable into elementary arrangements of names with simple meanings starts to falter. And since, as we saw in Chapter 1, the idea that meaning is simple is intimately connected to the idea that sense is determinate, the latter too starts to falter. Soon, Wittgenstein finds himself questioning whether the sense of propositions really is determinate in the way specified by the *Tractatus*. If it is not, then meaning and sense are not the precise, sharply demarcated items he believes them to be in the *Tractatus*, and logical analysis may not be as useful to philosophy as he suggests in that book.

By the time he is giving his 1930–1933 lectures, Wittgenstein has become convinced of the need for a whole new approach to these questions. He spends the following decade developing this new approach. We are going to spend the remainder of this chapter considering this new approach to philosophy and to language, as it emerges in what is generally regarded as the most important text from this period: the *Philosophical Investigations* (which I will also sometimes refer to just as the *Investigations*).

In Summary

– The following two ideas are central to the *Tractatus*: the idea that concepts have essences (i.e. fixed, clearly demarcated sets of essential features) and the idea that logical analysis is a central tool for clarifying concepts.

– A concern over the logical independence of elementary propositions initiates a process that eventually brings the entire conceptual edifice of the *Tractatus* down. This process culminates in the development of an altogether new approach to philosophy and to language, one that finds its clearest expression in the *Philosophical Investigations*.

iii. CONCEPTS WITHOUT ESSENCES: THE NOTION OF FAMILY RESEMBLANCE

By the time Wittgenstein comes to write the *Philosophical Investigations*, his entire approach to philosophy has undergone a radical transformation. Although he still regards his task as a philosopher to be primarily one of conceptual clarification, his understanding of what this involves is altogether different. In the *Tractatus*, clarifying an ordinary concept (such as that of bachelor) involves logically analyzing it: it involves breaking it down into increasingly precise propositions; ultimately this process is intended to deliver elementary propositions – propositions that belong to a highly precise, purely logical language, one totally unlike the natural languages we ordinarily use. Logical analysis is therefore a process that takes us further and further away from ordinary language. Clarifying concepts, in this view, involves moving away from the accidental features characteristic of our natural languages and homing in on the essential features of concepts, features which are best revealed in the purely logical language of elementary propositions.

This understanding of what is involved in clarifying a concept is totally abandoned by the time Wittgenstein is writing the *Philosophical Investigations*. Instead of moving deeper and deeper into logical analysis, Wittgenstein urges us to stay at the level of ordinary language and '*look*' at the way in which language is used there. Wittgenstein suggests that as soon as one starts to consider how ordinary language is used, one comes to realize that concepts do not, for the most part, have essences. For the most part, concepts do not have a rigid set of essential features. In order to illustrate this point, Wittgenstein uses as an example the concept of a game. The passage of the *Investigations* that discusses this idea is very revealing of Wittgenstein's new philosophical method and style. He writes:

Consider for example the proceedings that we call "games". I mean board-games, card-games, ball-games, Olympic games, and so on. What is common to them all? – Don't say: "There *must* be something common, or they would not be called 'games'" – but *look and see* whether there is anything common to all. – For if you look at them, you will not see something that is common to all, but similarities, relationships, and a whole series of them at that. To repeat: don't think, but look! – Look for example at board-games, with their multifarious relationships. Now pass to card-games; here you find many correspondences with the first group, but many common features drop out, and others appear. [. . .] Is there always winning and losing, or competition between players? Think of [the card game] patience. In ball-games, there is winning and losing; but when a child throws his ball at the wall and catches it again, this feature has disappeared. [. . .] (PI 66)

The idea here is that there isn't one set of features common to all games: there is no one set of features that is essential to all of the activities we call 'games'. In fact, there isn't even *one* feature (let alone a *set* of features) that is essential in this way. The concept of 'game' covers a collection of activities that resemble each other in various respects, but which don't all share any one, essential characteristic. There might be features that some games share with each other; but there is no one feature that *all* games share with each other. This is true even if one thinks of really general features. For instance, some board-games share with some card-games and with some ball-games the feature of involving competition between players – but not all of them do. Similarly, some games share with each other the feature of there being a winner – but not all of them do. The card-game called 'patience' does not involve competition between players; the game a child might play of throwing a ball against a wall involves neither competition between players nor the notion of there being a winner.

The idea that there isn't one feature in common to all games may seem very counter-intuitive. A common reaction when faced with it is to try to think of more features, perhaps increasingly general ones, in the hope that one of them will fit the bill. For instance, we might think: what about enjoyability? Is this not something that all games must share in common if they are to be games? Is this not, therefore, an essential feature of all games? Or: how about the fact that games have to be played by living creatures? A human being, a cat even, can be said to play a game – but a rock cannot. Isn't the fact that game participant(s) have to be alive an essential feature of games? In fact, however, neither of these features are common to all game-playing. Two computers can be said to play a game against each other – for instance, a game of chess. Yet computers (at least to date!) are neither alive nor capable of enjoyment. The more we think about it, the more we find ourselves forced to concede that there is no one feature common to everything we call a game. Some games share characteristics with each other, but there is no one feature common to *all* games. The concept of a game involves, instead:

> a complicated network of similarities overlapping and criss-crossing: sometimes overall similarities, sometimes similarities in detail. (PI 66)

Wittgenstein goes on to conclude:

> I can think of no better expression to characterise these similarities than "family resemblances"; for the various resemblances between members of a family: build, features, colour of eyes, gait, temperament, etc. etc. overlap and criss-cross in the same way. – And I shall say: "games" form a family. (PI 67)

So there is no one feature (or set of features) common to everything that falls under the concept of 'game'. Instead, games share with each other features that intersect and overlap. Consider how features are shared by the following three games: football; the child's solitary game of making a ball bounce against a wall; and the card-game called 'patience'. Football shares with the child's solitary ball-game the fact that a ball is involved, but not the number of participants; 'patience' shares with the child's game the fact that they both involve one player, but not the fact that a ball is involved; football shares with patience the idea of there being such a thing as winning and losing, a feature that is not shared by the child's game, etc. This is similar to the way in which physical features are distributed among the members of a family: Peter and Anna share their hair colour in common; Anna and Joyce the shape of their mouths; Peter and Joyce the colour of their eyes, etc. There is no one feature in common to the three of them – only a pattern of overlapping features. That is all that is needed for us to speak of there being a family resemblance between Peter, Anna and Joyce.

Wittgenstein does not suggest that all of our concepts are family resemblance concepts. But he does believe that many of our concepts – notably, as we will see shortly, concepts such as those of 'language' and 'proposition' – *are*. Still, there remains a strong resistance to the idea that *any* of our concepts should be family resemblance ones. Surely, we insist, there must be *some one thing* that we mean when we speak of 'games'. Surely there must be some feature circumscribing the way in which we use this concept. Otherwise, how is it that we all understand what we are talking about, when we talk of 'games'? What else – other than this one feature (or set of features) – could we all be talking about when we talk of games? The urge to look for the essences of concepts – the urge to look for the feature or set of features common to all instances of a concept – is very deep in us. Wittgenstein acknowledges this. Indeed, he notes that this urge is at the root of many apparently intractable problems in philosophy. For the later Wittgenstein, these problems result from mistakenly assuming that there must be an essence (a set of essential characteristics) to the concept under consideration. In this respect, he regards himself as having contributed to the problems of philosophy by writing the *Tractatus*, since this book has a strongly essentialist bent. It is partly in order to combat our strong urge to look for the essences of concepts that he starts the *Investigations* by discussing what has come to be known as the 'Augustinian picture of language'.

iv. THE AUGUSTINIAN PICTURE OF LANGUAGE

Instead of beginning the *Philosophical Investigations* with a description of his new philosophical method, Wittgenstein begins with a demonstration – by applying his method directly. Part of the idea here is that the best way to convey his new philosophical method is simply to show how it works in practice, rather than to try to describe or explain it. From the beginning, therefore, the *Philosophical Investigations* is conceived not just as an argument, but as a set of examples designed to train us into a new way of practising philosophy.

The *Investigations* begins by presenting one particular view of language: the view defended by St Augustine (hence the 'Augustinian picture of language'). Wittgenstein chooses this view specifically because it happens to contain many of the assumptions that fuel our – and his own earlier – urge to look for the essences of concepts. We are going to look at these assumptions in more detail in a moment; for now, let us see why Wittgenstein is so keen to engage with them.

Many of these assumptions are to do with how language works. Notice indeed that, in the previous section, when we were trying to articulate the reasons for insisting that the concept of 'game' must have an essential feature, we immediately turned to making certain assumptions as to how language works. We asked: how could we all understand what we are talking about, when we talk of 'games', if there is no feature in common to all games? And: what – other than this feature – could we all be talking about when we talk of games? These questions carry implicit *assumptions about language*: assumptions about the way in which language functions and what makes it possible. Augustine's account of language is interesting to Wittgenstein because it expresses many of the assumptions that lie behind our urge to look for the essences of concepts. Some of these assumptions are ones that Wittgenstein himself made in the *Tractatus* (and which he now thinks of as misguided). Others, although not part of the *Tractatus*' view, remain interesting to Wittgenstein because they help to explain our search for essential features. In critically dissecting Augustine's account, Wittgenstein therefore hopes to dispel many of the assumptions that prevent us from embracing the notion of family resemblance. Augustine's view therefore provides him with the starting point for a discussion with an invaluable, imaginary interlocutor – an interlocutor capable of articulating the very objections and assumptions that are blocking our way. By dealing thoroughly with these objections, Wittgenstein hopes to 'cure' us of the urge always to search for the essential features of concepts – an urge that is at the root of the most deeply entrenched philosophical problems.

The *Philosophical Investigations* begins, then, by identifying some assumptions implicit in Augustine's view of language – assumptions that Wittgenstein hopes to dispel. In this chapter, we will take a closer look at Wittgenstein's treatment of three of these assumptions, namely:

(i)   Language is uniform
(ii)   The meanings of words are taught by means of ostension
(iii) All words have objects as their meanings

Let us just cover briefly what is meant by each of these.

According to Augustine, language is uniform in that *all* of language is the same and works in the same way. There is, in this respect, *one* essence (one set of essential features) common to all language – an idea that is very much shared by the earlier Wittgenstein, in the *Tractatus*.

The second assumption implicit in Augustine's view of language is that the meaning of words is taught by means of 'ostension' – that is, by pointing at objects in the world. Augustine's view is that we teach the meaning of words to each other by pointing at objects while repeating the appropriate word (PI 6). So, for instance, I might teach a child the meaning of the word 'tree' by pointing to a tree and repeating: 'tree', 'tree', 'tree'. This process eventually enables the child to understand the meaning of the word 'tree', so that she or he can go on to use it correctly in other contexts. According to Augustine, all of the words in language are taught to us by means of ostension. This view, it must be said, does not appear to be a part of the *Tractatus*. The *Tractatus* does not really discuss the question of how we go about learning a language. In fact this question would have been regarded by the earlier Wittgenstein as one relating to *mechanisms*: here, the mechanism that happens to enable us to acquire language. As we saw earlier, however, questions relating to mechanisms are the purview of the natural scientist, but they are of no real interest to the philosopher, for the earlier Wittgenstein. Talk of mechanisms is irrelevant to the earlier Wittgenstein, because mechanisms are not part of what is *essential* to a concept, and Wittgenstein's aim, in the *Tractatus*, is to bring out the essences of concepts. Once Wittgenstein abandoned the idea that concepts had essences, questions concerning mechanisms became worth exploring again. In the *Investigations*, Wittgenstein suggests that examining Augustine's notion of ostension and considering the question of how we think language might be learnt helps us become clearer as to the concept of language itself. We will see shortly how this plays out.

Augustine's third assumption is that words have objects as their meanings. This is of course reminiscent of the *Tractatus*' view that the meanings of names are objects. However, Augustine's notion of meaning differs from the *Tractatus*' in at least one important respect: the objects that give meanings to our words, for Augustine, are ordinary, everyday objects we can perceive through our senses – objects such as trees and chairs, even animals and human beings, not the simple meanings that are Tractarian objects. Augustine's view implies, for instance, that the meaning of the word 'tree' is a tree (one of those woody, leafy things we see when we go for a walk in the park). Or that the meaning of the word 'John' is the man, John. The tree and the man both count as objects in this view: they are the meanings of, respectively, the words 'tree' and 'John'.

Augustine's notion of an object and of what counts as meaning is therefore different from (and a good deal more straightforward than!) the *Tractatus*'. In the *Tractatus*, ordinary words (such as 'tree', 'John', etc.) do not have meanings; only the names that emerge at the ultimate level of analysis do. For the earlier Wittgenstein, ordinary words (such as 'tree', 'John', etc.), when they are used to express a proposition, can be analyzed into further propositions with senses – an analysis that continues all the way to the level of elementary propositions. Tractarian objects are the meanings of the names that emerge at this ultimate level of analysis: the names that make up elementary propositions. Tractarian objects are nothing like the objects we come across in ordinary life; they are not the things that we see and touch. They are simple meaning units that are only revealed to us once propositions are completely analyzed. Augustine's objects, in contrast, are not simple in the way required by the *Tractatus* and they are readily available to us without the need for logical analysis: we can see them and touch them in the ordinary way.

Although Augustine's notion of an object is clearly very different from the *Tractatus*', the two views coincide in that they both present meaning as essentially *object-based*. In both views, the notion of meaning is best captured by focusing on the notion of object (even though the objects in question are very different in each case). This idea – the idea that the notion of meaning is best captured by focusing on the notion of object – is one on which Wittgenstein had a complete change of heart. Part of the aim of the *Investigations* is to undermine it, as we will see in this chapter.

Wittgenstein regards these three assumptions implicit in Augustine's view – language is uniform; ostension is central to language acquisition; meaning is object-based – as central to traditional philosophy. He recognizes that he himself fell prey to two

of them (the first and the third), in the *Tractatus*: such is the hold
these views have on us that Wittgenstein himself was taken in by
them, even though he was at a time working hard at trying to rid
philosophy of conceptual confusion! Doing away with these three
assumptions is crucial, however, since these assumptions are at
the root of many apparently unsolvable problems in traditional
philosophy. These problems are like diseases of philosophy: if we are
to cure philosophy of its ailments, it is essential that we do away
with the assumptions that give rise to them. In this respect, the
Investigations (and, indeed, the *Tractatus*) can be seen as having a
strongly therapeutic dimension.

In Summary

– Wittgenstein chooses Augustine's account of language as his
  target in the *Philosophical Investigations* because it incorporates
  three assumptions that are central to traditional philosophy.
  (i)   The assumption that language is uniform. According to
        Augustine, all of language works in the same way and there
        is such a thing as an essence to language.
  (ii) The assumption that language acquisition involves a process
        of ostensive pointing. I can teach the meaning of the word
        'tree' by pointing at a tree while repeating the word 'tree'.
  (iii) The assumption that meaning is object-based. For
        Augustine in particular, the meaning of the word 'tree' is a
        tree – that is, an object we can perceive through our senses.
– Wittgenstein says these assumptions have a very powerful hold
  on us. They are the basis of much traditional philosophy.
  Wittgenstein himself fell prey to the first and (to a version of)
  the third in the *Tractatus*, in spite of his determination to do
  away with conceptual confusion. It is important to eradicate
  these assumptions because they are at the root of many
  apparently intractable philosophical problems.

v. LANGUAGE-GAMES AND THE UNIFORMITY ASSUMPTION

Having teased out the assumptions in Augustine's view of language,
Wittgenstein moves to dismantling them. His method for undermining
these assumptions involves using what he calls 'language-games'.
Wittgenstein introduces the notion of a 'language-game' in Section 7

of the *Investigations*, but he never gives us a definition of the term. This is far from an oversight: Wittgenstein insists that no such definition can be given, in that giving a definition involves giving the essential features of something and there are no essential features to language-games.

In a moment, we will consider some of the language-games examined by Wittgenstein in the *Investigations*. Before we do so, however, it is worth saying a little more about this notion. Although it is not possible to give a definition that captures a set of (essential) features common to all language-games, it is, I think, useful to give a very general approximation to the term. Very broadly, language-games are sections of language that can be used as examples to illustrate the idea that language is a *purposeful activity*. Language-games help us see that language is an *activity* we engage in – an activity with a *purpose*. Most importantly, for Wittgenstein, they also help us see that different areas of language are used for very different purposes: there is no one single purpose served by all areas of language. Some of the language-games Wittgenstein considers in the investigations are invented: we will call these fictional language-games. Others are drawn from real life, they are sections of the language we use ordinarily: we will call these non-fictional language-games. Fictional and non-fictional language-games are both used by Wittgenstein to throw light on the concept of language and, in so doing, to chip away at the three assumptions belonging to the Augustinian view. Throughout Part I of the *Investigations*, Wittgenstein is in dialogue with an imaginary interlocutor who speaks on behalf of the Augustinian camp. By systematically replying to the objections from this Augustinian interlocutor and by relying on the use of language-games, Wittgenstein hopes to do away with our deep-seated urge to think about language in the way Augustine does.

Wittgenstein begins in PI (1) by questioning the assumptions that language is uniform and that all meaning is object-based. He does so by means of a fictional language-game involving a shopkeeper. In order to make the most out of Wittgenstein's example, think of this language-game as if it really were a game: a game to do with language, one involving three players. Wittgenstein describes the language-game of the shopkeeper in the following way:

> I send someone shopping. I give him a slip marked "five red apples". He takes the slip to the shopkeeper, who opens the drawer marked "apples"; then he looks up the word "red" in a

table and finds a colour sample opposite it; then he says the series of cardinal numbers [. . .] up to the word five and for each number he takes an apple of the same colour as the apple out of the drawer. (PI 1)

Wittgenstein uses the language-game of the shopkeeper to emphasize the idea that language is not uniform – more specifically, the idea that words do not all function in the same way. The words written on the paper slip function in very different ways in this example. The word 'apple' instructs the shopkeeper to pick fruit from the apple drawer; the word 'red' instructs the shopkeeper to check a colour sample; the word 'five' instructs him to say the series of cardinal numbers up to five while picking an apple with each number. Words can have very different functions in language. What's more some words do not seem to stand for objects at all: they just do not seem to have objects as their meanings. The word 'apple' could in this example be said to stand for an object – that is, for an apple; but the word 'five' cannot: 'five' does not seem to be about an object, in the way that 'apple' seems to be. The word 'five' enjoins the shopkeeper to count, not to look for the object *five*.

Language is not uniform – more specifically, it is not the case that all words in language have object-based meanings, as Augustine suggests. As well as words like 'five', think of words like 'of', 'can', 'which', 'any', etc. none of which can be said to indicate or point to an object of any sort, yet all of which are vital instruments in the function of language – indeed, all of them have formed part of this sentence. The question then becomes: does at least *some* of language behave in the way described by Augustine? Perhaps Augustine's theory applies to some areas of language – perhaps it applies, not to *all* of language, but to *most* of language or to the *most important* parts of language. In that case, Augustine's account would retain its importance, even if its scope had been reduced. In order to explore this idea, Wittgenstein turns to a different language-game: the language-game of the builders. He describes the language-game of the builders as follows:

Let us imagine a language for which the description given by Augustine is right. The language is meant to serve for communication between a builder A and an assistant B. A is building with building-stones: there are blocks, pillars, slabs and beams. B has to pass the stones, and that in the order in which A needs them. For this purpose they use a language consisting of the words 'block', 'pillar', 'slab', 'beam'. A calls them out; – B brings the stone which he has learnt to bring at such-and-such a call. (PI 2)

In this section, Wittgenstein asks us to imagine a tribe whose entire language consists of four words: 'block', 'pillar, 'slab' and 'beam'. The children of this tribe are taught to bring the appropriate building-stone when one of these four words is called out. We are also told that these children learn the meaning of these words by means of ostensive teaching:

> The children are brought up to perform *these* actions, to use *these* words as they do so, and to react in *this* way to the words of others.
> An important part of the training will consist in the teacher's pointing to the objects, directing the child's attention to them, and at the same time uttering a word; for instance the word 'slab' as he points to that shape. [. . .] (PI 6)

According to Wittgenstein, the language of this tribe of builders is simple enough to be a good candidate for meeting Augustine's description. After all, this language seems suitably object-centred (its four words – 'block', 'pillar, 'slab' and 'beam' – all relate to objects); and it seems suitably based on ostension, since we are told that the children of the tribe learn their language by a process of ostensive teaching. On the surface, it therefore looks like the language of the builders fits Augustine's description.

In fact, however, it does not. Consider, for instance, the question of how, precisely, ostensive teaching is supposed to help a child learn the language of this tribe (PI 6). According to the Augustinian theory, teaching this language involves repeating the words in that language, while ostensively pointing to an appropriate object. So, for instance, the teacher might repeat the word 'slab' while pointing to a slab. By the end of this process the child should, in the Augustinian view, have understood the meaning of the word 'slab'. What, exactly, counts as understanding the meaning of the word 'slab'? Well, for Augustine, the child can be said to understand the meaning of the word 'slab' when a mental image of a slab comes up before the child's mind whenever he or she hears the word 'slab' (almost like a kind of Pavlovian response to the stimulus of the word!). In other words, understanding the meaning of a word involves coming up with the appropriate mental image when one hears the word (PI 6). When the teacher ostensively points to a slab while repeating the word 'slab', the child comes to understand the meaning of the word 'slab' because an image of the slab comes before his or her mind.

Wittgenstein asks us to consider whether this account is correct. Does understanding the meaning of the word 'slab' involve having a mental image of a slab? He suggests that, in order to answer this question, we need to consider what the purpose of this word is in this language. In this language, the purpose of the word 'slab' is to elicit a certain reaction. The language is set up in such a way that, if you say 'slab!' to me, I am meant to react by bringing you a slab. If instead I remain still (perhaps inwardly dwelling on some fascinating mental image of a slab), you would consider that I haven't really understood how 'slab' functions in this language: I have not really come to grips with the meaning the word has in this language. In effect, in the language of this tribe, the word 'slab' has the function of a command: saying 'slab' in this language is analogous to us saying 'bring me a slab!' Understanding the meaning of the word 'slab' in this language involves reacting, upon hearing it, by going to fetch a slab. If I just sit there contemplating a mental image, I am not playing my part in this language properly.

Now, there may very well be other languages in which the appropriate response, upon hearing certain words, is just to try to conjure up appropriate mental images. We could play a game in which whenever one of us says 'slab' the other players are meant to form a mental image of a slab. In this other language-game, understanding the meaning of the word 'slab' would involve coming up with a certain type of mental image – that is, a mental image of a slab. But – and this is Wittgenstein's key question – why should we assume that meaning always functions in this way? Generally, we would be better off saying that understanding the meaning of a word involves acting – or reacting – *in an appropriate way*: in the language-game of the builders, it involves reacting by going to fetch an object; in the language-game about mental images, it involves conjuring up a certain mental image.

According to Wittgenstein, emphasizing the notion of *action* helps to undermine the idea that the meaning of words is taught by means of ostensive pointing. In order to see this clearly, we can look again the language-game of the builders. In this language-game, understanding the meaning of the word 'slab' involves going to fetch a slab. Can the meaning of the word 'slab' be taught by means of ostensive pointing? Can I get a child to understand the meaning of the word 'slab' by pointing to slabs while repeating the word 'slab'? It seems I cannot. No amount of pointing and repeating the word 'slab' is going to teach a child to *bring* a slab when the word is called out – and to understand 'slab', in the context of *this* game, is to bring a slab when the word is called out. A child who learns to participate fully in this language-game would have to learn not just the concept of a slab; he or she would also have to grasp the picking up and bringing, the handing-over, the whole interchange. It would seem, then, that something is left unaccounted for in a simply Augustinian account of how the language of the builders is learned.

> Am I to say that [the ostensive teaching] effects an understanding of the word? Don't you understand the call "Slab!" if you act upon it in such-and-such a way? – Doubtless the ostensive teaching helped to bring this about; but only together with a particular training. With different training the same ostensive teaching would have effected a quite different understanding. (PI 6)

In Wittgenstein's view, what counts as understanding meaning depends on which language-game (or which area of language) one is working in. It is distorting to suggest that learning or understanding meaning always involves the conjuring up of *mental* images. Language is not uniform. In fact it is the opposite of uniform – it is highly heterogeneous. There is an astonishing variety and range of real and fictional language-games, and what counts as 'understanding meaning' differs widely across them. Ostensive learning and mental picturing might – conceivably – have a role to play in certain areas of language, but certainly not in all areas. This idea is explored in PI 23:

> But how many kinds of sentence are there? Say assertion, question, and command? – There are *countless* kinds: countless different kinds of use of what we call "symbols", "words", "sentences". And this multiplicity is not something fixed, given once for all; but new types of language, new language-games, as

we may say, come into existence, and others become obsolete and get forgotten. (PI 23)

Language is an *activity* and there are countless varieties of *acting* that count as language:

> Here the term 'language-game' is meant to bring into prominence the fact that the *speaking* of language is part of an activity, or of a form of life.
>
> Review the multiplicity of language-games in the following examples, and in others:
> Giving orders and obeying them –
> Describing the appearance of an object, or giving its measurements –
> Constructing an object from a description (a drawing) –
> Reporting an event –
> Speculating about an event –
> Forming and testing a hypothesis –
> Presenting the results of an experiment in tables and diagrams –
> Making up a story; and reading it –
> [. . .]
> Translating from one language into another –
> Asking, thanking, cursing, greeting, praying. (PI 23)

Language is an activity: it is first and foremost about *acting* in certain ways, rather than, for instance, about *thinking* in certain ways. And language is an activity with *purpose*. What is important is to recognize that there is no one purpose in common to all areas of language, just as there are no actions required by all areas of language. The purpose, when you are playing the game of giving orders and obeying them, is very different from the purpose when you are playing the game of reporting an event. Similarly, what counts as having understood is very different in both games. And the two games involve different actions, different ways of acting. Imagine that you and I are playing the game of giving orders and obeying them – or, to put it differently, imagine that we are both engaged in this area of language. My purpose, if I give you an order, is to elicit a certain reaction from you: the reaction of obeying my order. You will count as having understood my order (assuming that you are willingly engaged in this game) if you act in a particular way, that is: if you do indeed obey my order. Understanding the words in this language involves acting in certain ways: either by giving orders (a speech act) or by obeying them (by performing the actions ordered). Now imagine that you and I are playing the game of reporting an event – or, to put it differently once more, that we are both engaged in the area of language that is to do with reporting events. Your purpose here is to make reports that I can understand. And I will count as having understood your reports if I can rephrase key sections of them, or if I can expand appropriately on what you said. For instance, imagine that you report 'it is cold and raining today'; I will count as having understood your report if, for instance, I expand on this by saying: 'We will need to take our coats and umbrellas if we go out'. This reply is a valid move in this language-game: it shows that I have understood your report. Another valid move might be for me to say 'let's go out nevertheless' and then proceed to fetch our coats and umbrellas.

Different areas of language require different types of actions and have different purposes. Indeed, what counts as understanding language can vary widely in different areas of discourse. Although language is a purposeful activity, there is no one purpose in common to all areas of language (to all language-games) – nor is there one set of actions common to all. There is no one essence in common to all that is language. Language is not uniform, it is not homogeneous. It is, on the contrary, radically heterogeneous. It is therefore emphatically not as Augustine initially suggests.

In Summary

- Wittgenstein uses language-games in order to undermine Augustine's view of language.
- Language-games are sections of language (fictional or real) that can be used as examples to emphasize the idea that language is a *purposeful activity*. Language is first and foremost about *acting* in certain ways (rather than about thinking); and it is about acting with a purpose.
- The language-games of the shopkeeper and of the builders are used by Wittgenstein to undermine the uniformity assumption. They are used to show that different sections of language involve different actions and have different purposes. Understanding

language involves acting in different ways: what counts as understanding language depends on the area of language (on the language-game).

– The language-game of the builders also shows that Augustine's emphasis on ostensive teaching is not appropriate to every area of language. Areas of language that are primarily about giving orders and obeying them (such as that of the builders) cannot be taught by pointing at objects and repeating words. In these areas, understanding what is being said – that is, understanding an order – involves acting in a particular way – that is, it involves acting in such a way as to obey the order. This is what counts as understanding what has been said, when one is engaged in this area of language. For this reason, this area of language cannot be taught by a process of ostension alone.

vi. NAMING AND OSTENSION

Wittgenstein's discussion of the language-game of the builders aims to show that the Augustinian account of language does not fit *all* language. What is involved in teaching and understanding language varies depending on the area of language we have in mind. For instance, ostension (the process of pointing at an object while repeating a word) cannot, by itself, teach someone to fetch a slab when the order 'slab!' is called.

At this point in the discussion, the Augustinian interlocutor comes up with a new strategy. This strategy involves conceding that not all of language fits Augustine's account, while insisting that the account accurately portrays one really important area of language: the area that relates to names and naming. In other words, the strategy of Augustine's defender consists in giving up the uniformity assumption (the view that all language works in the same way), while arguing that one really fundamental area of language – that of naming – does fit Augustine's other assumptions: names do have objects as their meanings and the meanings of names are taught by means of ostension.

By 'names' here we do not mean names in the complex, Tractarian sense – Wittgenstein has abandoned that line of thinking by this stage. What is meant here is what we might call words that refer to things and qualities. This would include proper names like Peter, Anna and Molly and also what in philosophy we call 'general terms'.

For instance, 'red' is a general term: it is the name we give to redness in general. Similarly 'cat' is a general term: it is the name we give cats in general. The main difference between proper names and general terms is that proper names pick out one particular individual, whereas general terms cover entire types, entire classes of individuals. For instance, imagine that Anna and Molly are the proper names of two cats. We might say 'Anna the cat' (when speaking of Anna) or 'Molly the cat' (when speaking of Molly). 'Cat' is a general term, a name that covers cats in general; 'Anna' and 'Molly' are proper names that pick out individual cats.

In the Augustinian view, all names (i.e. all proper names and general terms) have meanings as their objects and are such that their meanings are taught by means of ostension. So I might teach you a proper name by pointing to one particular cat while repeating 'Anna'. Alternatively, I might teach you the meaning of the general term 'cat' by pointing to one cat (say, Anna) and repeating the word 'cat', and then pointing to another cat (say, Molly) and repeating the word 'cat', and then pointing to yet another cat and repeating 'cat', etc. Teaching the meaning of general terms is more complex as a process than teaching the meanings of proper names (it involves pointing at lots of different cats!). In both cases, however, teaching meaning involves pointing at objects while repeating words: it involves ostension, according to Augustine.

Wittgenstein's first – and perhaps strongest – objection consists in pointing out that any ostensive pointing can be misinterpreted. Imagine, for instance, that you are trying to teach a child the meaning of the general term 'red' by pointing to a red object, say a red book, and repeating 'red'. The child might, for instance, end up thinking that the word 'red' means book, or made of paper. The problem is that the gesture of pointing to the red book can be interpreted in many different ways – and can therefore be misinterpreted. This is not just a problem when it comes to general terms such as the term 'red'. Even in the apparently more straightforward case of proper names, such as 'Peter', the same problem arises. Imagine that I point to my friend Peter while repeating 'Peter'. The listener could end up thinking that by 'Peter' I mean the colour of Peter's shirt, or the fact that Peter is a man, or the fact that he is walking when I happen to point at him.

The Augustinian interlocutor responds at this point by introducing the notion of an ostensive definition. An ostensive definition is a more sophisticated form of ostensive process. For instance, rather than merely pointing at an object while repeating a word on its own, I might use a whole sentence. For instance, I might say 'this word means *this*' while pointing at a cat; or we might say '*this* [pointing at a cat] is called a cat'. The idea here is that I can teach the meaning of names by using sentences of a certain type while pointing at an object. The advantage of this approach is that the sentences in question can be made to be quite precise: the hope is that this increased precision might eliminate the vagueness that comes from simply pointing and repeating a word. In fact, however, this notion of ostensive definition does not resolve Augustine's problem, in Wittgenstein's view. Wittgenstein dedicates Sections 26 to 38 of *Philosophical Investigations* to showing this.

One of the first points that Wittgenstein makes about ostensive definitions is that, because they too involve pointing (albeit pointing accompanied by a sentence, rather than merely by a word), they suffer from the same problems as the more basic ostensive processes. Saying '*This* is called Peter' while pointing (rather than merely repeating the word 'Peter' while pointing) doesn't much help the listener:

> He [the listener] might equally well take the name of a person [the name 'Peter'], of which I give an ostensive definition, as that of a colour, of a race, or even of a point of the compass. That is to say: ostensive definition can be variously interpreted in *every* case. (PI 28)

To this, the Augustinian interlocutor replies that it might be possible to solve this problem by giving more precise or more detailed ostensive definitions. For instance, I might say 'This man is called Peter', thereby signalling that my pointing is not meant to pick out a colour, or a species, or a point in space, but one particular man. Similarly, in the case of pointing at the red book, I might say 'This *colour* is called red', thereby indicating that my intention is to pick out the *colour* of the book, not the fact that it is a book or that it is made of paper or that it is solid. However, ultimately, this does not solve the problem, in Wittgenstein's view. The reason for this is that adding 'man' or 'colour' to one's ostensive definition only helps the listener if she or he *already* grasps the meanings of the words 'man' and 'colour'.

Wittgenstein is quick to point out the two main ways in which this is an intractable problem for the poor Augustinian. First, he reminds us that some of the words that make up ostensive definitions are not themselves candidates for being taught by means of ostension. Imagine trying to teach someone the meaning of the word 'this' by pointing. How exactly would that work? What would you point at? Secondly, he suggests that, even if by some miracle all of the words in ostensive definitions could be taught by means of further ostensive definitions, there would remain a serious problem. Consider again the ostensive definition 'this colour is red' – let us call it OD1. Now, let us assume, for the sake of argument, that all of the words in OD1 can themselves be taught by means of further ostensive definitions (although, as we have just seen, they really cannot). In order for me to understand OD1, I would need to understand all of the words that make it up: I would need to understand the meanings of 'this', of 'colour', of 'is' and of 'red'. If the meanings of these words are taught to me by means of ostensive definitions, however, I also need to know the meanings of all of the words in these further ostensive definitions – let us call these further ostensive definitions OD2, OD3, OD4, OD5. But, for *this* to work, I would need to understand the words in all of the ostensive definitions in OD2, OD3, OD4, OD5, etc. etc. In other words: in Augustine's view, my understanding of the ostensive definition 'this colour is red' relies on my prior understanding of a very, very long chain of ostensive definitions.

Wittgenstein points out that this chain cannot extend infinitely – it must have a beginning. There must be some word that I learn *first*. But that first word must therefore be one that I did *not* learn by a process of ostensive definition (or we would continue extending our chain of definitions still further). In this scenario, therefore, I do not yet know the meanings of *any* words: I am, after all, trying to learn the meaning of my very first word (PI 29). How do I learn the meaning of my first word according to the Augustinian model? Well, by means of the more primitive process of ostension: the process that involves someone pointing at the object while repeating a word (rather than a sentence). But this process, as we saw earlier, is particularly prone to misinterpretations – there is no guarantee that I will learn what my pointing, repeating teacher intends me to learn. What is worse, such misinterpretations would then carry over through the entire chain of ostensive definitions: they would infect (as it were) my entire language. It is unlikely that I would be alone in this, either: the scope for error would be so great that it would be in practical terms impossible for everyday language to function at all if it were so widely open to misinterpretation and confusion. In

Wittgenstein's view, ostension cannot possibly be the foundation for our practice of naming things. If it were, it would be unlikely bordering on the miraculous for anyone ever to understand what other people are saying.

In Summary

–   Wittgenstein has already established that there are many areas of language in which the meanings of words cannot be taught by means of ostension. He now turns to the question of whether ostension – in particular, the more precise ostensive definitions involving whole sentences – are central to teaching us the meanings of *names* (that is here, proper names and general terms).
–   Wittgenstein shows that ostension, in and of itself, cannot be the foundation for our entire practice of naming. The basic ostensive process of pointing at an object while repeating a word is radically prone to misinterpretations. Although giving more precise ostensive definitions (ones involving whole sentences) does seem to help in this respect, ostensive definitions cannot account for how we learn *our first words*. Augustine's view therefore entails that we must learn our first words by the more basic process of pointing and having single words repeated to us. But that process is hopelessly misinterpretable and any misinterpretations, at that fundamental level, would come to infect our entire language – so much so that communication would be rendered effectively impossible.

vii.   MEANING AND USE

For the later Wittgenstein, all that is needed in order to learn the meaning of a word is to observe how this word is used by those who have mastered the section of the language (the language-game) in which the word features. Observing how words are used in language is both necessary and sufficient to learning their meanings: it is necessary in that one cannot learn the meaning of a word without observing how it is used; and it is sufficient in that observing the use of a word is all that one needs, in order to learn its meaning. Learning the meaning of a word involves learning as it were a move in the language-game (in the section of language) in which that word is used. And, in order to learn the moves of a game, all that one really needs is to observe the game being played.

Wittgenstein homes in on this idea with his chess analogy, in PI 31. In this section, he asks us to consider what might be involved in learning what the king is in chess. Wittgenstein acknowledges that ostensive definitions might play *some* role in this area, but he maintains that their role will always be minor. In order to see this, imagine that you are trying to learn what the king is in chess and that I say 'this is the king', pointing at one of the figures. This ostensive definition may be of some use to you if you already know how chess works and all you need to know is which of the figures on the board plays the role of king. However, no ostensive definition will teach you what the role of the king is within the game: an ostensive definition will not teach you how the king is *used* in chess. In Wittgenstein's view, learning how the king is used (learning the role of the king in chess) involves observing games of chess being played. He writes:

> When one [shows] someone the king in chess and says: "This is the king", this does not tell him the use of this piece – unless he already knows [how the game works] up to this last point: the shape of the king. You could imagine his having learnt the rules of the game without ever having been [shown] an actual piece. [. . .]
>
> "This is the king" (or "This is called 'the king'") are a definition only if the learner already 'knows what a piece in a game is'. That is if he has already played other games, or has watched other people playing 'and understood' – *and similar things*. [. . .]
>
> We may say: only someone who already knows how to do something with it can significantly ask a name. (PI 31)

Wittgenstein uses chess as an analogy for language, with the king piece standing (roughly) for a word in language. The idea is that learning the meaning of a word involves learning a set of *moves* in the section of language (in the language-*game*) to which the word belongs: learning the meaning of a word involves learning how the word is *used* in that section of language. (Similarly, learning the role of the king involves learning what moves one can make with this piece: it involves learning how this piece is *used* in chess.) Ostensive definitions (and, more generally, ostension) may have some small role to play, but they certainly do not have the major, fundamental significance that the Augustinian view ascribes to them.

So we have seen that understanding the meaning of a word involves knowing how the word is used in language. You count as having understood a word when you are able to make the right moves with it in the section of language to which it belongs: when you are able to use it in an appropriate way. Learning the meaning of a word is therefore akin to developing an ability or a skill: it involves acquiring an ability to use the word in a particular way. For this reason, ostensive definitions (and more generally ostension) cannot be central to teaching and learning a language; for no ostensive definition can give you the ability to *use* the word in the appropriate manner. What you need, if you are to master the meaning of a word, is training into the practice or the activity of using that word. Wittgenstein holds that this training can only come from observing how the word is used in language.

One of the consequences of this view is that it reveals Augustine's third assumption – the assumption that meaning is object-based – to be mistaken. According to Wittgenstein, the meaning of a word is not an object. The meaning of a word is the way in which the word is used in language. This emerges as part of his discussion of ostension. Imagine that you are new to the world (as it were!) and that someone is trying to teach you the meaning of the word 'red' by pointing at red things and saying 'red' (or 'This is red'). And imagine that, on this occasion, you happen not to misinterpret their gestures of pointing, so that, in each case, you pick out the right 'object': whenever they point at red things, you pick up on their *redness*, rather than some other feature of the red things such as the fact that they are solid. Still, picking the right object (here the *redness*) will not teach you how the word 'red' is *used* in language: it will not teach you that you can say 'this red is brighter than that red' but not 'this ball is red and green all over at the same time'. Correctly identifying the object that is being pointed at as part of an ostensive process is not the same as grasping the meaning of a word. There is more to the meaning of words than mere objects: the meaning of a word is the way in which a word is *used* in language.

In Summary

- Learning the meaning of a word involves learning how to use the word in. the area of language (in the language-game) to which the word belongs. Ostensive definitions (and, more generally, ostension) can only play a minor role in this respect.

- Learning the meaning of a word is akin to being trained into a practice of using the word in particulars ways. It involves developing an ability to make certain moves, with the word, in the language-game (in the section of language) to which the word belongs.

- One learns the meaning of a word by observing how the word is used in the area of language to which it belongs. Observing how the word is used in language is necessary and sufficient to learning the meaning of that word.

- There is more to the meaning of words than mere objects. The meaning of a word is the way in which the word is used in language.

- Wittgenstein therefore rejects Augustine's second and third assumptions: he rejects the idea that meaning is object-based; and he rejects the idea that ostension is central to teaching and learning the meanings of words.

viii. CONCLUSION

Wittgenstein uses the beginning of the *Philosophical Investigations* to show that Augustine's account of meaning misrepresents language. His strategy consists in identifying and undermining three assumptions implicit in the Augustinian view (that language is uniform; that ostension and ostensive definition are central to teaching and learning the meaning of words; and that the meanings of words are objects). He does so by using language-games and other examples, such as the chess analogy.

We have looked in this chapter at Wittgenstein's critique of all three of these assumptions. Wittgenstein argues, first of all, that language is not uniform. In his view, there is no such thing as the essence of language. Language lacks a distinct, unifying nature. A set of phenomena is called 'a language', not because all of these phenomena share one feature (or set of features) in common, but because they are related in a very particular way: they form a family. Language is a family resemblance concept.

Instead of producing something common to all that we call language, I am saying that these phenomena have no one thing in common which makes us use the same word for all, – but that they are related to one another in many different ways. (PI 65)

Having dissected the first assumption, Wittgenstein goes on to reject Augustine's second assumption, that ostension is central to learning the meanings of words. The problem here is not simply that there are sections of language in which ostension cannot play a central role (for instance, the language-game of giving orders and obeying them). It is that ostension cannot play a central role even in the area of naming. I cannot teach the meaning of a name (a proper name such as 'Peter' or a general term such as 'red') by pointing and repeating the name in question, because this process can be fundamentally misinterpreted. And I cannot resolve this problem by introducing more precise ostensive definitions (such as 'This colour is red') because they cannot account for how we learn our first words.

Having questioned the role of ostension in the learning of meaning, Wittgenstein moves against Augustine's third assumption. He argues, contrary to Augustine, that the meanings of words cannot be objects. For there is more to meaning than can be captured by the notion of an object. Indeed, identifying an object does not, by itself, give you the meaning of a word. Grasping the meaning of a word is knowing how to use the word correctly in language. The meaning of a word is therefore the way in which the word is used in language. Words are used in a wide variety of ways in language: grasping the meaning of a word is therefore something that can only be achieved by observing how the word is used in the area of language to which it belongs.

CHAPTER 5

RULES AND MEANING

i. INTRODUCTION

In the previous chapter we saw that, for the later Wittgenstein, meaning is use. The notion of *use* is central to Wittgenstein's accounts of what it is for a word to *have* meaning, of what is involved in *learning* the meaning of a word and of what counts as having *understood* the meaning of a word. The meaning of a word is the way in which the word is used in language. You learn the meaning of a word by observing how the word is used in the section of language to which it belongs. And you count as having understood the meaning of a word (you count as having learnt it) when you use it correctly in that section of language.

In this chapter, we will be looking at Wittgenstein's discussion of one important objection to his later view on meaning. This objection consists in saying that meaning must be something *in the mind*, rather than being merely the way in which words are *used*. Part of the thinking behind this objection is that it is in fact possible for me to use a word correctly without having really understood its meaning. For example, I might be able to pass myself off as having understood an unfamiliar word simply by parroting the manner in which other people use it. Perhaps I have recently read a poem in which a pool of water is described as 'limpid'; the next time I come across a pool of water I might say, 'Ah, what a limpid pool', no doubt impressing my friends but still with no actual understanding of whether what I have just said means that the pool is deep, or cool, or wet, or fresh, or any of the other things a pool of water might be. (So long as the pool happens to be clear and not muddy, I have nevertheless apparently used the word correctly.)

This would seem to suggest that using a word correctly is not, in and of itself, enough. If you are to count as having genuinely understood the meaning of a word, surely there must in addition be something going on in your mind: you understand the meaning of the word when the meaning comes (as it were) 'before your mind's eye'. Let us call this view that meaning is something in the mind the 'mind-based model of meaning'.

The mind-based model of meaning may seem quite persuasive. It looks pretty obvious that there *is* a difference between using a word (even correctly) and understanding its meaning. I *can*, after all, simply mimic what others say: I can copy how they use words without understanding what these words mean. I can even write a simple computer program to combine nouns, verbs, adjectives and so forth into meaningful sentences, without the computer that assembles them having any comprehension of what is going on – of what the 'meaning' of those sentences is. And, surely, since what is missing in these cases is *understanding*, what is missing is something *mental*, something going on in the mind. From this, it may seem natural to conclude that understanding the meaning of a word involves having this meaning in one's mind: I count as having understood the meaning of a word if I have, as it were, mental access to it – if the meaning is present in my mind. The meaning of a word is therefore, in this view, a *thing* that comes before my mind. But what kind of 'thing' is it?

Wittgenstein discusses two important mind-based models of meaning in the *Philosophical Investigations*: one of them relates to the notion of rule; the other to that of sensation. In this chapter, we will consider the former; in the next chapter, we will examine the latter. In this chapter, therefore, we are going to focus on a particular mind-based model of meaning, one that turns essentially on the notion of a rule. In this model, the meaning of a word is not the use this word has in language, but the *rule* that governs this use – what is more, this rule is essentially something in the mind, it is something mental. As we will see in Section ii, Wittgenstein attacks this account in two stages: first, he argues that not all areas of language are governed by rules; secondly, he argues that even those areas that are rule-governed are misrepresented by this mind-based account of rules. In Section iii, we will revisit Wittgenstein's view that meaning is use in the light of his discussion of rule-following.

In Summary

–   Wittgenstein considers a mind-based objection to his view that meaning is use. The objection runs as follows. There is a difference between using a word correctly and genuinely understanding the meaning of that word. In using the word correctly, I might be simply mimicking what others do, without any understanding of what the word means. It seems that what is missing, in this scenario, is something mental: the understanding. The conclusion therefore appears to be that meaning is not use: meaning is instead something in the mind. Wittgenstein disagrees with this and spends part of the *Investigations* criticizing this view.

ii. RULES, MIND AND MEANING

In the previous chapter we saw that, for Wittgenstein, learning the meaning of a word is learning how to *use* the word correctly in the section of language to which it belongs. Mastering language is, in this respect, analogous to mastering the playing of a game – so much so that Wittgenstein calls the various sections of language 'language-games'.

Let us consider again the analogy that Wittgenstein draws with the game of chess. Part of the aim of this analogy is to emphasize that learning the meaning of a word involves learning a set of *moves* in the section of language (in the language-game) to which the word belongs – just as learning the role of the king in chess involves learning what moves one can make with this piece (how this piece is *used* in chess). According to Wittgenstein, we learn the meanings of words by observing how words are used in language – similarly, we learn what the king is in chess by observing how the king piece is used in games of chess. Understanding the meaning of a word involves using the word correctly in language, just as we might use a chess-piece correctly in the course of a game.

You may by this stage be feeling a sense of unease about all this. Part of this unease might come from the idea that, surely, one can understand what the king is in chess without ever using the king piece. In fact, I can understand what the king is in chess without ever having played a game of chess, and therefore, without having ever used *any* of the chess pieces. I can read a rule book, or have the game explained by a friend; I need never even have seen a chessboard so long as someone has described it to me accurately enough. It would seem that I can 'learn the game' without ever having been exposed to it, let alone having played it. This would appear to suggest that use is not, after all, as central as Wittgenstein would have us believe. In that case, however, we need to look elsewhere for what might be involved in understanding what the king is in chess. And, as soon as we start looking elsewhere, we start to be drawn to the notion of rules – and, from this notion, to that of a *mental* rule: a rule that is present before the mind.

Let us consider, therefore, the following, alternative version of what might be involved in understanding the role of the king in chess: that we understand what the king is in chess if we grasp the *rule* that describes how the king is used in chess and that this rule is something mental, something in the mind. In order to see more clearly the notion of rules at the heart of this view, let us imagine the following scenario. Imagine that a chess-playing championship is taking place in a big hall and that, on the walls, there are signs that describe in an exhaustive manner the various uses of the chess pieces (the various moves one can make with these pieces). Imagine also that, whenever there is a technical dispute as to whether or not a certain move is allowed in chess, the players consult these signs in order to settle the dispute. Since these signs describe exhaustively the ways in which the pieces are used in chess (since they leave nothing out), the disputes can always be settled by reference to them.

Rules, in this view, are very much like these signs – the difference being that they are signs inside our minds. Why do they have to be 'inside our minds'? Well, we need to remember that this model emerges from a concern that use is not enough: use has to be accompanied by understanding and understanding (this model claims) is something that goes on inside the mind. The idea here, then, is that learning what the king is in chess must involve *internalizing*, in some sense, the signs that are hanging on the walls: it must involve bringing these signs into our minds, paying attention to them inwardly when appropriate and storing them in there for future reference. If the sign is physically hanging on a wall in front of you, but you do not pay attention to it (if it does not end up 'in' or 'before' your mind), then you would not have a genuine understanding of the game of chess. Grasping a rule, in this view, therefore involves having something similar to the physical sign, but having it inside your mind:

it involves having a mental sign that describes the way in which the king is used in chess. And it is having this mental sign that determines whether or not you have understood *what the king is* in chess.

One of the advantages of this view is that it explains how it is possible for me to understand what the king is in chess without having ever actually used the king piece in a game of chess. In other words, understanding what the king is does not necessarily involve actually using the king piece; instead it involves having before one's mind the *rule-sign* that describes the way in which this piece is used. Conversely, if you use the king piece correctly but do not have this sign before your mind, you cannot be said to genuinely understand what the king is in chess: you may be mimicking the way in which others use the king piece, or you may have made a legitimate move by complete random chance, but in either case you do so without genuine understanding.

So, how does this talk of rules translate into the discussion of meaning? Well, in this model of meaning, understanding the meaning of a word involves grasping the rule that describes the various ways in which the word is used in language – and this rule is a mental sign: it is a sign that comes before the mind. As we have just seen, this has the implication that you can understand the meaning of a word without ever actually using the word in language. Conversely, you can use a word correctly without understanding its meaning. Use, in this view, is no longer central to the understanding of meaning. What determines whether or not you genuinely understand the meaning of a word is not whether you use the word correctly, but whether you have the appropriate rule (the appropriate mental sign) before your mind. Likewise, the meaning of a word is not the use of a word; it is the rule (understood as a mental sign) that describes that use. Unsurprisingly, this leads to a different understanding of what is involved in learning the meaning of a word. Instead of asking a pupil to *observe* how words are used by others, the teacher may simply present the pupil with a physical sign that describes the use of the word: for instance, one of the physical sign hanging on the walls in the chess tournament. The pupil can be said to have genuinely learnt the meaning of the word when this physical sign is, as it were, internalized: when the corresponding mental sign (or mental rule) comes before the pupil's mind.

That, then, is the rule-based account of meaning. As I mentioned earlier, Wittgenstein believes this account to be profoundly mistaken.

And yet, the idea that linguistic meaning consists, first and foremost, of *rules* might seem very appealing. We may even feel that Wittgenstein is in danger of shooting himself in the foot by drawing an analogy between language and games. After all, it might be thought that, if there is one thing that *is* common to all games, it is that they are all governed by rules. If language is game-like, then, surely it makes sense to say that rules are central to linguistic meaning.

Wittgenstein does not think so, however. In order to see why, he asks us to consider the wide range of phenomena we call 'playing a game'. He suggests that, as soon as we do this, we come to realize that not all instances of game-playing *are*, in fact, governed by rules. He writes:

> We can easily imagine people amusing themselves in a field by playing with a ball so as to start various existing games, but playing many without finishing them and in between throwing the ball aimlessly into the air, chasing one another with the ball and bombarding one another for a joke and so on. [. . .] And is there not also the case where we play and – make up the rules as we go along? (PI 83)

The lesson, as we saw in the previous chapter, is that there is no essence in common to all game-playing, just as there is no essence in common to all language. 'Game' and 'language' are family resemblance concepts. Some instances of game-playing are governed by rules; others are not. We can amuse ourselves by playing a ball game that involves making the rules up as we go along – but that game will, of course, not be governed by a definite set of rules: it will not be governed by a set of rules that describes what to do *in all of the situations we might face while playing this game*. Similarly, for Wittgenstein, word use need not be governed by rules in order for it to count as meaningful language. It is *not* the case, in his view, that:

> [. . .] if anyone utters a sentence and *means* or *understands* it he is operating a calculus according to definite rules. (PI 81)

> [. . .] a word is not everywhere bounded by rules. (PI 81)

This is the first stage in Wittgenstein's reply to the rule-based objection. It consists in noting that not all sections of language are governed by rules. In order to clarify this, it is worth considering again what Wittgenstein means by a rule here. As we saw before, a rule is here a mental sign that describes, exhaustively, all of the ways in which a word (or a chess piece) is used. According to Wittgenstein, not all areas of language are governed by such definite, exhaustive rules. In fact, in most areas of language, we use words without there being a rule that covers all possible contingencies. Wittgenstein asks us to imagine the following scenario:

> I say 'There is a chair'. What if I go up to it, meaning to fetch it, and it suddenly disappears from sight? – [I might then say:] 'So it wasn't a chair, but some kind of illusion'. – But [imagine that] in a few moments we see it again an we are able to touch it and so on. – [Then, I might say:] 'So the chair was there after all and its disappearance was some kind of illusion.' – But suppose that after a time it disappears again – or seems to disappear. What are we to say now? Have you rules for such cases – rules saying whether one may use the word 'chair' to include this kind of thing? But do we miss them when we use the word 'chair'; and are we to say that we do not really attach any meaning to this word, because we are not equipped with rules for every possible application of it? (PI 80)

The crucial point Wittgenstein is making here is that we use the word 'chair' without there being a definite rule that covers (exhaustively) all possible scenarios – such as this one. What matters here is not whether any one has ever experienced a situation such as this one. This is, after all, an invented example. What matters is that this is a *possible* scenario. It is possible – in the sense of *conceivable*, imaginable – that someone might have such an experience: it is part of the concepts we have. And yet, we do not have a definite rule that covers whether or not we should use the word 'chair' in this situation. In other words, we use the word 'chair' without there being a rule that covers, exhaustively, all possible contingencies. And yet, it is clear, according to Wittgenstein, that we regularly use the word 'chair' meaningfully. There are therefore areas of language that are not governed by definite, exhaustive rules. In fact, Wittgenstein goes as far as suggesting that most areas of language are not governed by such rules.

So, not all of language is governed by definite, exhaustive rules of the type we discussed above. This is the first prong of Wittgenstein's attack on the rule-based account of meaning. The second prong of

Wittgenstein's attack consists in showing that even those areas of language that *are* governed by definite rules do not behave in the way that the model suggests. Wittgenstein is happy to concede that *some* areas of language – for instance, some areas of mathematics – are governed by definite, exhaustive rules. However, he also argues that the mind-based model of rules we have discussed above misrepresents what is involved in following a rule in these areas. In order to see what he means here, let us consider how the mind-based model of rules might fare in, for instance, the area of addition.

What, we may ask, is involved in understanding the meaning of the expression 'to add'? According to the mind-based model of rule-following, I only count as having understood the meaning of 'to add' if a certain rule is present before my mind. More specifically, I only count as having understood the meaning of 'to add' if there is, before my mind, a mental sign that describes all of the ways in which this expression is used. In this view, therefore, I only genuinely understand the meaning of 'to add' when this rule – this mental sign – is present before my mind. If I use the expression 'to add' correctly and this sign is present before my mind, then I am genuinely following the rule of addition and I can be said to understand the meaning of the expression 'to add'; if I use it correctly without this sign being present before my mind, then I do not really understand the meaning of 'to add' – I may just be mimicking others without genuinely understanding what they are saying.

According to Wittgenstein, this mind-based model of rule-following is profoundly unsatisfactory. Its main problem comes from the fact that the model equates understanding or grasping a rule with attending to a *sign* (here, a mental sign). Think back to our discussion of ostension in the previous chapter. There we saw that, for Wittgenstein, the gesture of pointing at an ordinary object can be radically misinterpreted. Imagine that I am trying to teach you the meaning of the word 'red' by pointing to a red book. If you are totally new to English, if you really have no idea what kind of a word 'red' is, my pointing to a red book will be utterly unhelpful to you: you might end up thinking that 'red' means book (or man-made, or some particular area of space, or even the action of pointing!). Wittgenstein believes that, as soon as we conceive of rules as mental *signs*, we open the way for a similar difficulty.

Imagine that you have absolutely no idea what chess is, but that you are standing in the chess-competition hall, wondering what on earth everyone around you is doing. And imagine that someone draws your attention to a sign on the wall that describes the way in which chess pieces are used: the king does this, the queen does that, if the king is in this situation then . . ., if the queen is in that situation, then . . . etc. Now, the problem is that the sign, in and of itself, can be interpreted in many different ways. If you *really* have no idea what chess is, paying attention to the sign will not, in itself, help you to understand it – it will not help you to interpret it correctly. You might read it and draw the conclusion that sign is an avant-garde poem or some kind of complex riddle. *Attending to* the sign is not the same as *understanding* the sign – and it is certainly not the same as understanding the rules of chess. Imagine now that you have an amazing photographic memory, so that you are able to conjure up, in your mind, a perfect mental copy (or mental image) of the physical sign hanging on the wall. Does paying attention to this (mental) sign – inside your mind – entail that you understand the rules of chess? Again, the answer seems to be: no. The mere fact that the sign is now 'inside your mind' does not really make a difference. *Attending to* a sign – whether it is a physical sign that you see through your eyes or a mental image that you 'see', as it were, by looking inside your mind – is not the same as understanding it.

Part of the problem here is that the mind-based account of rules presents rules primarily as signs that require an interpretation. Understanding a rule therefore becomes, in this view, primarily about 'hitting on the *correct* interpretation' of a sign. But paying attention to a sign, in and of itself, does not guarantee that you will hit on its correct interpretation. If you really have no idea what chess is, you may conclude that the sign hanging on the wall of the chess hall is a poem, or a riddle, or perhaps a description of the strange rules of engagement of two warring nations. In that situation, it may seem that what is needed is some further rule: a rule that tells you how to interpret the first sign, for instance, something like the rule 'the first sign describes a board game'. But then, this second rule is itself, in this view, a sign that requires an interpretation. In order to be sure that you are interpreting *it* correctly, you will need a further, third rule – and so on and so forth.

This leads to an infinite regress: understanding any one given rule requires understanding an infinite series of other rules; correctly interpreting any one sign requires correctly interpreting an infinite number of other signs. Just as in the case of ostension as a method of teaching meaning, this is eminently suspect. It is very difficult to see how anyone could ever be said to understand a rule or to interpret a sign correctly, if this infinite process is what is involved in so doing. Our conclusion then has to be either that this view is incorrect, or that we never actually understand a rule or correctly interpret a sign (in spite of all appearances to the contrary). Wittgenstein believes the former to be the case: in short, the view that says that understanding a rule involves attending to a sign that requires interpretation is conceptually confused.

Still, someone might object that perhaps the latter is the case: perhaps the model is correct and we never genuinely understand a rule or interpret a sign correctly (in spite of all appearances to the contrary). Wittgenstein rejects this suggestion, however, by considering the question of how, according to this model, we might come to understand and follow a rule *for the very first time*. Indeed, on that first occasion, there are no other rules to rely upon. On that first occasion, there is therefore nothing to *determine* the correct interpretation of the rule-sign. But, if there is nothing to determine this, then it seems that any interpretation of the rule-sign is equally acceptable. This can be put differently by saying that, in this scenario, there is nothing to determine how the rule should be applied, what its correct application is. But if there is nothing to determine the correct application of the rule, then *any* application of it is equally acceptable. *Anything* I do can be regarded as fitting the rule. This, surely, is paradoxical. After all, the very point of having rules is to draw distinctions between correct and incorrect moves – between correct and incorrect applications of the rules. If the mind-based account of rule-following leads to the collapsing of this distinction, there must be something profoundly confused about it (just as there was with the process of ostensive learning, which as we have seen fell foul of a very analogous set of problems). This is the conclusion Wittgenstein reaches in PI:

> This was our paradox: no course of action could be determined by a rule, because every course of action can be made out to accord with the rule. [. . .] if everything can be made out to accord with the rule, then it can also be made out to conflict with it. And so there would be neither accord nor conflict here.
>
> It can be seen that there is a misunderstanding here [. . .].
> (PI 201)

The model that presents rules as mental signs requiring interpretation leads to the collapsing of a distinction that is central to the notion of a rule: the distinction between correct and incorrect application. For Wittgenstein, this signals that there is something conceptually confused about this model: the model misrepresents the phenomenon of rule-following.

There must therefore be some other way to understand what is involved in grasping and following a rule. But what is it? How do we go about finding it out? Faced with these questions, we would do well to remember Wittgenstein's rejoinders in his earlier discussion of games: *'look and see* [. . .] don't think, but look!' (PI 66). Wittgenstein asks us to *look* at how we go about following rules and talking about rule-following in ordinary circumstances: it is by looking at ordinary cases of rule-following that we will succeed in clarifying the notion of a rule. In order to emphasize this point, Wittgenstein asks us to consider what is involved in following a signpost. Imagine that you have gone out for a walk in the countryside and that you want to get to a particular village. You come across a signpost on the road showing you the direction to this village and you start walking in the direction it indicates. What is involved in your following the signpost? Do you treat the signpost as something that requires an interpretation? Do you look at it, ponder how it should be interpreted and, having settled on one of several possible interpretations, start walking again? It seems not. When we come upon a signpost in the road, we do not look at it, stop to *interpret* what it might possibly mean, and then make a decision to act according to this interpretation. This description gives an overly cerebral cast to the entire situation. It portrays us as over-thinking things, whereas in fact, when we follow a signpost, we do so in a much more straightforward manner. According to Wittgenstein, when we come across a signpost, we simply act in the way we have been *trained* to act when faced with signposts: we act according to a *practice* we partake of.

[. . .] What this [shows] is that there is a way of grasping a rule which is not an interpretation, but which is exhibited in what we call 'obeying the rule' [. . .]. (PI 201)

[. . .] 'obeying a rule' is a practice. (PI 202)

Understanding and following a rule is not about hitting on correct interpretations. It is about taking part in a practice or *custom*:

> The words [. . .] "following a rule" relate to a technique, to a custom. (*Remarks on the Foundations of Mathematics*, VI, 43)

Crucially, for Wittgenstein, the practice or custom of following a rule is closer to that of *obeying orders* than to that of interpreting signs. This notion of obeying orders is one we have come across before. In Chapter 4, for instance, we saw that the language-game of the builders is made up exclusively of orders: the cry 'slab!', in that game, is equivalent to the order 'bring me a slab!'; the cry 'block!' to the order 'bring me a block!'; etc. As we saw then, in those areas of language that are primarily about giving orders and obeying them, understanding what is being said – understanding the order – involves acting in a particular way: it involves acting in the way we have been trained to act when we are presented with that order. Understanding the order 'slab!', for instance, involves bringing a slab to the person who has called out the order. The case of rule-following is similar, according to Wittgenstein. Understanding a rule involves acting in a particular way: it involves acting in the way we have been trained to act when presented with that rule.

The notions of practice, custom and training are crucial to Wittgenstein. In fact, they are central to explaining not just the phenomenon of rule-following, but also that of hitting on the correct interpretation of a sign. In order to see this, consider two games, both of which make use of the same series of cards – cards that show people acting in various ways: running, skipping, crawling, etc. (These games are not discussed by Wittgenstein but they serve to illustrate the point.) In the first game, one of the players has a pair of headphones on which songs are being played; when a song begins, this player chooses the card they think will best convey the title of this song and shows it to the other players. So, for instance, if the song playing on the headphones is called 'Run', this player might choose the card that shows someone running. The other players take turns in trying to guess the title of the song until one of them makes the right guess: that is, until one of them says the title of the song that is being played on the headphones. Let us call this the guessing game.

The second game is quite different. Here, the first player holds up a card and the other players have to imitate the action portrayed in that card. So, for instance, if the first player chooses the card that shows someone running, the other players have to start running. Whenever someone gets tired and stops running, they are 'out'. The last person left running wins and gets to choose the card next time round. Let us call this the action game. Both games involve one player choosing a card and showing it to the others; but, in each game, the card is being used for two quite different purposes. In the guessing game, the running card is effectively being used as a sign that requires an interpretation. Indeed, this game is all about hitting on the correct interpretation of the card: it is about guessing what song the card is being used to represent. In the action game, the same card is being used for a very different purpose: it is used to give an order, namely the order 'run!'.

It is worth noting that the distinction between correctness and incorrectness is preserved quite naturally in both of these examples. The distinction emerges in two different ways: first, there is, in both examples, a clear distinction between playing the game properly and playing it wrong; secondly, in each case, there is a clear distinction between winning and losing. If, in the middle of the guessing game, you start to imitate the actions shown in the card, you are playing the game wrong; conversely, if, in the middle of the action game, you stop and ponder what you should interpret the card as representing, you are playing that game wrong. Playing the guessing game properly involves trying to hit on the correct interpretation of the card, it does not involve performing the action shown by the card; conversely, playing the action game properly involves performing that action, it does not involve trying to hit on the correct interpretation of the card. There is a clear distinction between playing these games properly and playing them wrong. There is also a clear distinction between winning and losing. If you are playing the guessing game (i.e. playing it properly), then the winning move consists in saying the title of the song that is being played on the headphones. If you are playing the action game (properly), you win if you are the last person left performing the action shown by the card.

There are two conclusions to be drawn from these examples. The first is that the notion of practice is central both to the activity of interpreting signs correctly and to that of following rules. The second is that the practice of interpreting signs correctly is very different from the practice of following (or *obeying*) a rule: the two practices involve acting in very different ways. We will look at each of these points in turn.

Why is the notion of practice central to both rule-following and the activity of interpreting signs, for Wittgenstein? The reason is that, without there being an established practice, there would be no distinction between correctness and incorrectness at the heart of these phenomena. Consider again the guessing and action games. In both of these games, there is such a thing as playing the game properly and playing it wrong; and in both there is such a thing as winning and losing. In both games, this is possible because there is a *practice* in place: there is a practice as to what counts as playing these games properly; and there a practice as to what counts as winning and what counts as losing.

This notion of a *practice* was altogether missing when we first discussed what is involved in interpreting a sign. Earlier, we spoke as if we should be able to derive what counts as the correct interpretation of a sign from the sign alone: all we had was the sign itself and, from it alone, we were meant to work out how it should be interpreted. As we saw, however, this approach ends up collapsing the very distinction between a correct and an incorrect interpretation. The problem, according to Wittgenstein, is that this (crucial) distinction cannot be preserved if all we have is the sign by itself. Without the notion of a practice, the very idea of hitting upon the correct interpretation of a sign becomes impenetrably mysterious – it becomes incomprehensible, because the distinction between a correct and an incorrect interpretation dissolves. This was the lesson in Wittgenstein's discussion of what is involved in following a rule for the first time. As soon as one brings in the notion of practice, however, all this becomes a lot more straightforward. In the guessing game, hitting upon the correct interpretation involves saying the title of the song playing in the headphones. Why? Because that is the practice, that is the custom in that game: that, in other words, is what that game *is*. Similarly, with the notion of rule-following: to follow the rules of chess is to make certain moves in certain situations. Why precisely those moves? Because that is what is involved in the practice of chess playing. That is what the custom is. That's what *chess* is.

So, the first conclusion to be drawn from these examples is that the notion of *practice* is central to both the phenomenon of interpreting signs and to that of rule-following. The second is that, although the notion of practice is central to both, the practice of rule-following is very different from the practice of interpreting signs.

The practice of rule-following is closer to that of obeying orders than to that of interpreting signs: in this respect, the practice of rule-following resembles more the action game than the guessing game. A rule is a sign that is used to *command* a certain action. If a sign is being used as a rule, it is being used as a command, not as something that requires interpretation. Understanding and following (or obeying) the rule involves not considering several possible interpretations of a sign, but acting in a particular way. Understanding a rule involves acting in such a way as to obey the rule. What counts as acting in that way? Well, in order to answer that question, you need to look at the practice that pertains to that rule. What counts as obeying the rules of chess (the actions involved in obeying these rules) is determined by the practice of playing chess; what counts as obeying the rules of backgammon (the actions involved in obeying those rules) is different and is determined by the practice of playing backgammon.

Following a rule involves performing certain actions when one is playing chess and certain other actions when one is playing backgammon. There is no one set of actions that is essential (or common) to all instances of rule-following. Nevertheless, there are similarities between different cases of rule-following – enough similarities for rule-following to count as a family resemblance concept (PI 179). And the (family resemblance) concept of rule-following is closer to that of obeying an order than to that of interpreting a sign: the *practices* that fall under the concept of rule-following resemble more those that fall under the concept of obeying an order than those that fall under the concept of interpreting a sign.

In Summary

- Wittgenstein considers one particular version of the mind-based model of meaning: an account that centres on the notion of rules. In this account, the meaning of a word is the mental rule-sign that (exhaustively) describes the use of that word. Rules in this view are exhaustive and definite. They are mental signs that require an interpretation.
- Wittgenstein presents three main reasons for rejecting this view. First, he notes that not all areas of language are governed by definite, exhaustive rules. Secondly, he suggests that this understanding of rules leads to an infinite regress. Finally, he

shows that this notion of rules leads to the collapsing of a
crucial distinction: that between correctness and incorrectness.
–   Wittgenstein concludes that the phenomena of rule-following
    and of interpreting signs can only be understood against the
    background of an established practice. He also concludes that
    the practice of following rules is closer to that of obeying orders
    than to that of interpreting signs. We explored these ideas
    through the examples of the guessing and the action games.

iii.   MEANING REVISITED: THE NOTION OF PRACTICE

The arguments we have been looking at give Wittgenstein the
ammunition he needs to attack in a pretty comprehensive manner
the mind-based view of meaning that centres on rules. He entirely
rejects the idea that the meaning of a word is the mental rule-sign
that governs the use of that word. In his view, this mind-based view
of meaning makes two crucial mistakes. First, it mistakenly assumes
that *all* areas of language are governed by definite rules. Secondly,
it misrepresents what is involved in following a rule and, therefore,
it misrepresents those areas of language that *are* governed by
definite rules.

   According to Wittgenstein, language is nothing like so clear-cut; it
is instead a family-resemblance concept. There is no one essential
feature in common to everything that is language; instead, different
areas of language merely resemble each other sufficiently to fall
under one and the same concept – they resemble each other enough
for them all to be called 'language'. To be more specific, there is one
important respect in which different areas of language resemble each
other: they all feature some notion of correctness and incorrectness.

   Looking at this last remark, one might make the objection that, if
all areas of language make use of the distinction between correctness
and incorrectness, then this distinction should be regarded as an
essential feature of language. Perhaps, the objection continues, there
is an essence to language after all: perhaps the essential feature of
language is precisely that all language makes use of this distinction.
This is a misunderstanding, however. If there was one notion
of correctness and incorrectness running through all areas of
language, then, perhaps, the objection would be valid. However, in
Wittgenstein's view, what counts as the difference between a correct
and an incorrect move in the language game varies so widely across

different areas of language as to block the objection. All areas of language incorporate *some* notion of the distinction between a correct and an incorrect move; but what that distinction *is* – what counts as the difference between the two – varies so much that it is not possible to speak of one essential feature common to all language.

In order to see this more clearly, it is worth reminding ourselves of the wide variety of activities that count as language-games. Wittgenstein asks us to:

> Review the multiplicity of language-games in the following examples, and in others:
> Giving orders and obeying them –
> Describing the appearance of an object, or giving its measurements –
> [. . .]
> Reporting an event –
> Speculating about an event –
> Forming and testing a hypothesis –
> Presenting the results of an experiment in tables and diagrams –
> Making up a story; and reading it –
> [. . .]
> Translating from one language into another –
> Asking, thanking, cursing, greeting, praying. (PI 23)

What counts as the difference between correctness and incorrectness in these language-games varies widely. You are not playing the game of telling a story properly if you just repeat the same three words over and over again; in contrast, this might be a valid move in the language-game of praying, or in that or measuring objects (if, for instance, you are measuring cubes that are all the same size). In some language-games, the correct move might not involve *saying* anything at all at some key junctures: for instance, if you are playing the language-game of the builders we discussed in Chapter 4, the correct move, if you hear the cry 'slab!' is to bring that person a slab; it is not to *say* anything in reply. We can see therefore that, while it is the case that all language-games feature some distinction between correctness and incorrectness, what this involves differs so widely across them – the *practices* involved are so heterogeneous – that we cannot talk of there being one essential feature common to all of language. What counts as the distinction between correctness and incorrectness varies so much, that this distinction cannot be regarded as the one substantive feature that all of language has in common.

For Wittgenstein, teaching someone a language involves initiating them into a set of widely different – albeit interconnected – practices. It is important to note that a practice, in this context, is not necessarily the practice of a *community*. Wittgenstein is not suggesting that in order for me to follow a rule (or to interpret a sign) there must be some community (some group of people) setting the relevant standards of correctness and incorrectness. A practice *can* of course be the practice of a particular community or group of people – but it *need not be*. A practice (a custom) can just as well be the practice (or custom) of a single, solitary person.

Imagine that I am abandoned as a baby in a desert island and that I survive my ordeal. When I am older it so happens that the pack of cards from the example in Section ii washes up on the shore. I might, faced with these, develop a solitary version of the action game, where I pick a card at random and imitate the action it shows. This activity may not be much fun, if I am on my own without other people; but it would nevertheless be game with an established practice – a practice established in this instance by me. For something to count as a practice, there need not be more than one person involved; but the activity does need to happen more than once. Practices involve regularity and repetition: if you only do something once, you cannot speak of having established a practice or a custom. In the *Remarks on the Foundations of Mathematics*, Wittgenstein writes:

> Language, I should like to say, relates to a *way* of living.
> In order to describe the phenomenon of language, one must describe a practice, not something that happens once, *no matter of what kind*. (*Remarks on the Foundations of Mathematics*, VI, 34).

We might object here that we are not being told enough. Saying that language involves certain practices and that practices involve repetition and regularity seems to leave an awful lot of questions unanswered; it risks leaving us strangely unsatisfied. In fact, however, Wittgenstein thinks it is crucial to resist the temptation of trying to say more on this issue. One reason for this has to do with the view that language is a family resemblance concept. There is no one property that is common to everything that we call language, so language cannot be given one precise, unifying definition: it cannot be subsumed under one model (as, for instance, the rule-based model tries to do). Another reason for resisting the urge to continue asking for and giving explanations comes from the conviction that explanations must come to an end, that there is a point where explanations simply give out. On this issue, Wittgenstein writes:

> The difficulty here is: to stop. (*Zettel* 314)

> Why do you demand explanations? If they are given you, you will once more be facing a terminus. They cannot get you any further than you are at present. (*Zettel* 315)

If you really have no idea what language is, no descriptions or explanations that I or Wittgenstein could give you (in language!) would help. Your only hope would be for me to give you a certain type of training and thereby to bring you into the practice of using language. If you do already have a mastery of language, then certain explanations and descriptions might come in useful. If you have quite a good grasp of English but are unsure what 'bachelor' means, I might say to you 'a bachelor is a married man' and that might be of help to you. But there comes a point where descriptions and explanations give out. In fact, *it is part and parcel of the practice of using language* that there comes a point where they run dry.

> To what extent can the function of language be described? If someone is not master of a language, I may bring him to a mastery of it by training. Someone who is master of it, I may remind of the kind of training, or I may describe it; for a particular purpose; thus already using a technique of the language. [. . .]
> The difficult thing here is not to dig down to the ground; no, it is to recognize the ground that lies before us as the ground. (*Remarks on the Foundations of Mathematics*, VI, 31)

The idea that there is a point where explanations give out may seem suspiciously close to a cop-out. We might feel that the request for further explanations is a valid one and perhaps even that Wittgenstein refuses to comply because he cannot think of what else to say, rather than because of some well considered point. This would not be correct, however. The point that Wittgenstein is trying to make in the above remarks is rather obscure, but it is well considered and potentially persuasive. It can be put differently, by homing in on the idea that different areas of language constitute different language-*games*. Part of the idea here is that playing *any* game involves giving up our requests for certain explanations. You cannot play the game of chess if you spend your time questioning why the king piece moves in the way it does. Playing the game of chess involves not asking for such explanations – it involves giving up our requests for such explanations. That is what Wittgenstein is implying when he suggests that there is a point where explanations give out. It is part and parcel of the activity of game-playing (and therefore of the activity of language use) that there comes a point when we should stop asking for explanations and start to *act*.

In Summary

- Although Wittgenstein suggests that the distinction between correctness and incorrectness is central to all language, he maintains that there is no one feature in common to all language. Part of the reason for this is that what counts as a correct or an incorrect move in a language-game – that is, the practice involved – varies so much across language-games as to negate the idea of there being one feature in common to all of them.
- When asked for an explanation of this notion of practice, Wittgenstein replies that regularity and repetition are both central to it. He also emphasizes, however, that explanations give out at this stage.

iv. CONCLUSION

For Wittgenstein, the meaning of a word is the way in which that word is used in language. Learning the meaning of a word involves being trained into a practice: the practice of using that word in a particular way. And understanding the meaning of a word involves using the word correctly in language. Earlier in this chapter, we discussed the possibility that one might use a word correctly without really understanding it. This gave rise to the idea that understanding the meaning of a word must involve attending to something (specifically, a rule-sign) inside one's mind, rather than merely using the word correctly. Wittgenstein's discussion of rule-following shows, however, that attending to a sign that's present before your mind still does not guarantee understanding. The problem is not just that you may end up misrepresenting the sign that is before your mind; the problem is that the sign, in and of itself, is incapable of determining what its correct interpretation is. In fact, if all we have is the sign, the very distinction between a correct and an incorrect interpretation collapses.

For the distinction between correctness and incorrectness to be preserved, there has to be a practice at work: there has to be an established custom, a repeated and regular way of doing things. Language is the practice of using words in particular ways for particular purposes. There is, of course, an important difference between merely parroting the way in which others use a word (without any genuine understanding of it) and genuinely understanding the meaning of that word. But that very difference relies on there being a distinction between correctness and incorrectness; and *that* is reliant on there being a practice.

CHAPTER 6

SENSATIONS AND PRIVATE LANGUAGES

i. INTRODUCTION

In the previous chapter, we examined Wittgenstein's critique of one particular mind-based view of meaning. In this view, the meaning of a word is the *rule* that describes the use of that word and this rule is a *mental sign*: a sign that appears before the mind. Wittgenstein argues that this view of meaning is mistaken for two main reasons: the first is that not all areas of language are governed by definite rules; the second is that those that are so governed are in any case misrepresented by this mind-based view of rules. Wittgenstein notes that a rule, in this view, is a mental sign that requires an interpretation. For this reason, it is something that can be *misinterpreted* without some guidance as to how to interpret it. However, a rule-sign of this type, in and of itself, offers one no guidance of this kind – so much so that, if all we had were the sign itself, the very idea of there being a difference between a correct and an incorrect interpretation of the sign would vanish. This view of rules as mental signs requiring an interpretation makes it utterly mysterious how we could ever genuinely follow a rule. For Wittgenstein, rule-following can only be understood by referring to the notion of a practice; and the practice of rule-following is closer to that of obeying orders than to that of interpreting signs.

Wittgenstein's discussion of rule-following shows that the meaning of a word cannot be the mental rule-sign that describes the use of that word. The question we might be asking ourselves at this point is: should we conclude from this that meaning is *never* in the mind? In other words, even if we accept that the meanings of words are not mental *rule-signs*, we might be left wondering whether meaning could not be 'in the mind' in some other way. Well, there is one area of language that might give us particular pause for thought in this respect: the area of sensation language. Consider for instance the sensation of pain. Imagine that you kick me on the shin and that it causes me pain. If we were to unpack this occurrence further, we might say the following: there was a physical event (your kicking me) which caused a physical trauma in my shin which sent physical pain messages to my (physical) brain which, in turn, caused me to experience a *sensation* of pain. Consider a little more carefully what might be meant by 'sensation of pain' here. One way to explain what 'sensation' means in this instance would be to say that it is an internal *experience*. In this view, my sensation of pain – the inner experience or inner feeling itself – is a *mental* thing. Your kicking me on the shin is a physical event that starts a chain of physical causes and effects (the trauma in my shin, the messages sent to my brain, etc.). But this chain of physical causes and effects ultimately produces something mental: the experience, the sensation of pain.

In this view, therefore, the sensation of pain – the experience itself – is mental: it is in the mind. But it is a very different type of mental thing from the rule-signs we discussed in Chapter 5. The mental rules in Chapter 5 were signs that required interpretation and that could be radically misinterpreted: this is why they were ultimately unsatisfactory. My pain sensation, in contrast, does *not* stand in need of an interpretation in this way. Indeed, it would seem that I cannot really misinterpret it: if it seems to me that I am in pain, then, surely, I am in pain. Even if the sensation is a kind of 'phantom' pain caused by neural interference, with no physical trauma associated with it, it still feels just as painful to me: the sensation, the experience is there. In this respect, I am therefore in pain: after all, that is what being in pain is all about – it is about having a certain experience. *You* might misinterpret whether or not I am really in pain, but that is because you do not have access to what is going on inside my mind: you have to go by the way I act, and I may be choosing to conceal what I am really experiencing inside. But *I* cannot misinterpret my own sensation of pain. Another way of putting this would be to say that, for me, my sensation of pain is transparently what it is: it is not the kind of thing that requires interpreting and, by the same token, it is not something that can be misinterpreted.

In this view, therefore, sensations are mental things that cannot be misinterpreted by the person doing the experiencing: if it seems to me that I am in pain, then I *am* in pain. Sensations are therefore mental things that do not suffer from the shortcomings of mental rule-signs. The question for us is, therefore: could sensations play the role that mental rule-signs were not able to play? More specifically: could the meaning of the word 'pain', when I say 'I am in pain', be my mental sensation of pain? According to Wittgenstein, it could not. *Why* it could not becomes clear when one considers one of the consequences of the view: for this view leads to the notion that private languages are possible.

A private language, in this context, is something very specific. It is a language where the words have as their meanings things that can only possibly be known by the speaker. Imagine that I am experiencing a sensation (let us call it *S*) and that I say: 'I am experiencing S'. And imagine that only I can possibly have knowledge of my sensation *S*: only I can look inside my mind and have direct access to the sensation itself. If the meaning of the word 'S' is my sensation *S*, then only I can possibly know the meaning of the word 'S'. Now, imagine a language made up entirely of words such as 'S'. This would be a 'private language' in Wittgenstein's sense. It would be a language made up of words whose meanings could only possibly be known by the speaker.

In Wittgenstein's view, both the idea of a private language and the understanding of sensations associated with it are deeply problematic. In Section ii, we will consider more closely the relation between these two notions. In Section iii, we will examine Wittgenstein's critical discussion of them.

ii. PRIVATE LANGUAGES AND SENSATIONS

For Wittgenstein, a private language is a language made up of words whose meanings can only *possibly* be understood by one person: it is a language that others cannot *possibly* understand. A private language is not a language that simply *happens* to be understood by one person alone. Imagine, once again, that I am abandoned as a newborn in a desert island and that I survive. And imagine that, during my years in solitude, I develop a very primitive language in which I speak to myself: a language with ten words or so, say the words for different locations in the island, for the primitive tools I use, etc. Let us say that I even construct primitive propositions with these words, for instance the proposition that one of my tools is in a particular place in the island. Imagine now that a ship full of enthusiastic anthropologists arrives, that they start studying my language and that, eventually, they come to understand it. This language would not be a private language in Wittgenstein's sense. For it is not a language that other people cannot *possibly* understand: it is not a language that can only *possibly* be understood by me. This is a language that I *happen* to have developed on my own, in a situation of extreme solitude. For many years, I *happened* to be the only person who spoke and understood it. But it was always possible, in principle, for other people to understand it: indeed, when the ship full of enthusiastic anthropologists arrives, they are able to learn my language, they come to understand it. They may want to call my desert island language a *solitary* language – but it is not a *private* language in Wittgenstein's sense.

So a private language, as Wittgenstein has it, is a language that could not *possibly* be understood by anyone other than the speaker: the language is such that it is absolutely impossible for others to understand it. Wittgenstein believes that this notion of a private language causes a great deal of confusion, philosophically speaking; luckily he also believes it is one of those ingrained but deeply confused philosophical notions which disintegrates entirely when one pays careful attention to it. For Wittgenstein, a close examination of the idea of a private language exposes it for what it is – an inherently flawed pseudo-concept that should be discarded.

Wittgenstein believes that the notion of private language emerges from one particular way of understanding the mind – and sensations in particular. This view of the mind is implicit in the work of many traditional philosophers, but is perhaps most strongly embraced by the French philosopher René Descartes. Let us consider therefore what it is that Wittgenstein understands by Descartes' view of the mind (or the 'Cartesian' view, as it is often called).

For Descartes, the mind is a collection of essentially private states. The contents of my mind – my sensations in particular – are private to me, in a very strong sense. They are private to me in that only I can possibly know them. Imagine that I am experiencing the sensation of pain. Descartes believes that only I have *direct* knowledge of my pain because only I can look inside my mind and check that I am indeed experiencing pain. You may *believe* that I am in pain. If so, however, you will have inferred this *indirectly*, from my behaviour – but you cannot genuinely *know* that I am in pain. Wittgenstein writes:

I can only believe someone else is in pain, but I know if I am. (PI 303)

Conversely, in this view, only you have direct knowledge of your sensations, in that only you can look inside your own mind; I can only *believe* that you are in pain, indirectly, on the basis of how you behave, of what you say and do.

So, the first element in the Cartesian view of sensations is the idea that sensations are private to the person having them: only that person can possibly have *direct* knowledge of them. The second element in this view is that this direct knowledge is *infallible*. My direct knowledge of my sensations is infallible in that, if it *seems* to me that I am in pain, then I *am* in pain. The idea here is that it is impossible for me to make a mistake about my own sensations because, when it comes to sensations, there is no difference between how things *seem* to be and how they *really are*.

In order to unpack this a little further, consider a different type of knowledge, one in which the distinction between seeming and being is preserved. Consider my knowledge that there is a tree in the middle of the field. Say that I know this because I have repeatedly seen the tree through my window: I have seen birds flying to it, pecking at its fruit in the autumn, etc. My knowledge of the fact that there is a tree in the field is not infallible. It may seem to me that there is a tree in the field, without there really being one. In other words, it is *possible* for me to make a mistake in this area: I am not infallible here. Imagine for example that, without my knowing, the owner of the field recently cut the tree down and replaced it with a life-sized poster of the tree. The poster is placed in such a way that, from my window, it looks just as if the tree is still there. Clearly, this possibility is somewhat far-fetched (although that said, there are life-size concrete cows in the fields around Milton Keynes). But the important thing for us is that this is a *possibility*, it is conceivable or imaginable, however far-fetched it might be. In the case of my sensation of pain, this is not a possibility *at all*, according to Descartes. If it seems to me that I am in pain (in the sense of having the mental sensation, the inner experience of pain), then I *am* in pain (in that sense). When it comes to sensations – to inner experiences – there is no difference between seeming and being. I cannot make a mistake when it comes to my own sensations: my knowledge of them is infallible. Others, in contrast, are fallible in their judgements about my sensations. For instance, they may surmise, on the basis of my behaviour, that I am in pain, when, in fact, I am simply faking it. Other people's beliefs about my sensations can be mistaken; similarly, I can be mistaken about other people's sensations.

This notion of infallibility is quite subtle, so it is worth spending a moment on it. The idea is not just that I am infallible about the fact that I am having *some* experience – a sensation of some type. In Descartes' view, I am also infallible about the very *nature* of this experience: about the precise nature of my sensation. If it seems to me that my pain is a stabbing pain, then it is a stabbing pain; if it seems to me that it is a throbbing pain, then it is a throbbing pain. This, again, is different when it comes to my knowledge of the tree. Imagine that it seems to me that the tree in the field is a chestnut tree. And imagine that, on this occasion, there really is a tree in the middle of the field, but that it is not actually a chestnut, but a beech. In this scenario, I would be correct about *the fact that there is a tree* in the field, but mistaken about the *nature* of the tree. In other words, when it comes to my knowledge of the tree, I can be mistaken about the fact that there is *a* tree in the field (as in the earlier example with the poster) and I can be mistaken about the nature of the tree (as in this example). According to Descartes, when it comes to sensations, I can be mistaken about neither: I have infallible knowledge both about whether or not I am experiencing *some* sensation and about the *nature* of this sensation. Another way to put this point is to say that sensations are *transparent* to the person doing the experiencing: it is transparent to this person both that they are having some sensation and what the nature of the sensation is.

Sensations, for Descartes, therefore have two important characteristics: first, they are *private*, in that only I have direct knowledge of my own sensations (only I can access them directly by looking inside my own mind); second, I have *infallible* knowledge both of the fact that I am experiencing a sensation and of the nature of this sensation. Running through Descartes' entire approach to sensations (and indeed to the mind more generally) is a very strong conception of knowledge. In Descartes' view of knowledge, you can only be said to genuinely *know* something, if it is impossible for you to doubt that thing or to be mistaken about it. Indubitability (the inability to doubt) and infallibility are therefore central to the Cartesian view of knowledge. This is why only I can *know* that I am in pain; other people can *believe* that I am in pain, but I alone am in a position genuinely to know. The reason for this is that I alone am infallible about my sensations. Other people can doubt whether I am in pain and can be mistaken about it; for this reason, they cannot really be said to know that I am in pain. Knowledge is not compatible with the possibility of doubt or the possibility of mistakes.

Wittgenstein argues that the Cartesian notion of sensations fuels the idea of a private language. Indeed, if you start off with the Cartesian view of sensations, the move to the idea of a private language appears relatively straightforward – the Cartesian understanding of sensations invites or encourages the idea that a private language is possible. As we will see in Section iii, Wittgenstein thinks that both Descartes' notion of sensations and the notion of a private language are profoundly mistaken. Before we consider Wittgenstein's rejection of these notions, however, it is important to examine more closely why he thinks that the Cartesian view of sensations gives rise to the idea of a private language in the first place.

Wittgenstein asks us to consider the following account of sensation language – the following account of how language about sensations works. In this account, sensation words, such as 'pain', have as their meanings sensations inside our minds. So, for instance, when I say 'I am in pain', the word 'pain' has as its meaning my internal sensation of pain: the sensation inside my mind. In addition, in this account, words acquire their meanings by means of a process that is the mental equivalent to the ostensive process we discussed in Chapter 4. In Chapter 4, we discussed a view of language according to which the meanings of words are fixed and taught by means of ordinary ostension. In this view, I might teach you the meaning of the word 'tree' by physically pointing at a tree while repeating the word 'tree'. The account of sensation language we are currently considering adapts this notion of ostension and makes it into an internal, mental process. In order to explain this, let us consider the following example. Imagine that I have a sensation and that I decide to call it 'S'. How, we may ask, does the word 'S' acquire its meaning? Well, in the view under consideration, I fix the meaning of the word 'S' by focusing my attention inwardly on my sensation (by internally 'pointing at it', as it were) while repeating the word 'S' to myself. This process of internal pointing (this private act of mental ostension) would, in this account, be the basis for the meaning of the word 'S'.

The idea is that this mental version of ostension has a major advantage over the ordinary process of ostension we discussed in Chapter 4. In Chapter 4, we saw that Wittgenstein rejected the view that ostension can form the basis of meaning because any ordinary gesture of pointing can be radically misinterpreted. My gesture of pointing at the tree can be interpreted in a wide variety of ways; the gesture, in and of itself, therefore offers you no genuine guidance as to how to interpret it – it cannot be the means by which you learn the meaning of the word 'tree'. When it comes to sensations, however, things seem to be very different, because sensations, in the Cartesian view, are transparent to the person who is experiencing them. I simply cannot be mistaken about the fact that I am having a sensation nor about the nature of this sensation: I am infallible about my own sensations. Since it is impossible for me to misinterpret my own sensations, this view says, why should mental ostension not be regarded as the basis of meaning – at least when it comes to the meaning of sensation words?

The first thing to note is that a language made up exclusively of sensation words (where sensations are understood in the Cartesian way) and based on mental, private ostension would be a private language in Wittgenstein's sense. It would be a language in which the words have as their meanings sensations that can only be directly accessed by the experiencer. Imagine that I set up the meaning of the expression 'S' by inwardly pointing to one of my sensations while repeating 'S'. Since only I have direct and infallible knowledge of my sensations, only I could possibly know the meaning of the word 'S'. A sensation language made up of words whose meanings were all set up in this way would be a private language in Wittgenstein's sense. A private language, in this context, is therefore one in which:

i. Words have as their meanings sensations that are private and transparent to the person experiencing them.
ii. This person fixes and learns the meanings of these words by means of private, ostensive gestures.
iii. It is impossible for another person to understand this person's language.

Wittgenstein describes this idea of a Private Language in the following two passages from the book *Philosophical Investigations*:

The individual words in this language are to refer to what can only be known to the person speaking; to his immediate private sensations. So another person cannot understand the language. (PI 243)

I can give myself a kind of ostensive definition. – How? Can I point to the sensation? Not in the ordinary sense. But I speak, or write the sign down, and at the same time I concentrate my attention on the sensation – and so, as it were, point to it inwardly. (PI 258)

In Wittgenstein's view, as we will now see, the notion of a private language is profoundly problematic. Both this notion and the Cartesian notion of sensations from which it arises must, in his view, be rejected. In the next sections, we will see how Wittgenstein goes about explaining why.

In Summary

- A private language, in Wittgenstein's sense, is a language whose words can only *possibly* be understood by the speaker. It is a language that is *impossible* for other people to understand. By contrast a solitary language (as in the desert island example) is not a private language in the required sense, since it is in principle possible for other people to come to understand it.
- The Cartesian view of sensations suggests that sensations are private and transparent to the person who experiences them. My sensations are *private* to me in that only I have direct knowledge of them; other people can only infer indirectly, on the basis of my behaviour, that I am experiencing them. In addition, my sensations are *transparent* to me in that I am infallible about them. If it seems to me that I am experiencing a certain sensation, then I am experiencing it. It is not possible for me to be mistaken (to misinterpret) that I am having a sensation or what the nature of this sensation is.
- For Descartes, knowledge implies indubitability and infallibility. I can only claim to know something if it is impossible for me to doubt or make a mistake about it. This is why, in the Cartesian view, only I can *know* that I am in pain; other people can only *believe* that I am.

– The Cartesian view of sensations fuels the notion of a private language. For it paves the way for the view that sensation words have as their meanings sensations that are private and transparent to the person who experiences them. In this view, when I say 'I am experiencing S', the word 'S' has as its meaning something that only I can possibly know: my sensation *S*. A language made up exclusively of such words would be a private language, in Wittgenstein's sense. It would be a language whose words could only possibly be understood by me.

iii. WITTGENSTEIN'S CRITIQUE: KNOWLEDGE AND INFALLIBILITY

Wittgenstein's first line of attack against the notion of a private language focuses on Descartes' view that only I can know my own sensations. According to Descartes, statements about sensations are essentially reports of sensations; and sensations are both private and transparent to the person doing the experiencing. This, together with Descartes' very strong conception of knowledge, leads to the idea that only I can know that I am experiencing a certain sensation; other people can *believe* (correctly or incorrectly, but always indirectly) that I am in pain, but they cannot *know* that I am. In the Cartesian view, I can only be said to know something if it is *impossible* for me to doubt and to be mistaken about that thing. Given this conception of knowledge, only I can be said to know that I am in pain – others can doubt and make mistakes as to whether I really am or not. This, as we saw above, appears to make plausible the notion of a private sensation language: it fuels the idea that only I can really know the meanings of my sensation words.

In order to begin the process of undermining this viewpoint, Wittgenstein asks us to consider how we use the verb 'to know' in ordinary, everyday situations. Descartes suggests that I can only claim to know something when it is impossible for me to doubt or to be mistaken about that thing. To this Wittgenstein replies that, as soon as we consider ordinary knowledge claims, we realize that the reverse is in fact the case. In ordinary situations, we only claim to know things in those areas that *allow* for doubts and for mistakes. Part of the reason for this, according to Wittgenstein, is that knowing something involves being able to *justify* that something. And justifications only have a *purpose* – and therefore a place – in those areas of language that allow for the possibility of doubt and of making mistakes. This is a complex idea, so let us spend a moment making it clearer.

Let us start with an example. Imagine that I see my neighbour John trip over in the street: I see him fall on his knee and then lie on the ground, moaning and holding his knee. Ordinarily, in this situation, it would be perfectly legitimate for me to say 'I know that John is in pain': this would be a perfectly proper use of the expression 'I know'. Imagine that I start to walk towards John to offer some help and that a passer-by asks me why I am doing this. I reply 'John is hurt: I am going to help him'. If the passer-by expresses a doubt about John's state, I might add, perhaps a little rudely: 'Look, I *know* that he is hurt: I just saw him trip over and now he's lying on the ground moaning'. This feels like a natural response on my part: there is nothing jarring in my use of the verb 'to know' here. The passer-by is expressing doubt as to whether John is in pain; in response to this *doubt*, I state that I *know* that John is in pain and then *justify* my knowledge statement by referring to John's behaviour (the fact that he tripped over and that he is now lying on the floor moaning). Doubt, knowledge and justification are all part of this scenario. In fact, they seem to go hand in hand. I make my knowledge claim and give my justification *precisely because* the passer-by is expressing a doubt: my claim to know and the justification that follows it have a *purpose* here precisely because there has been such an expression of doubt.

Imagine that the passer-by then tells me that, in fact, John is a compulsive joker: that he is always pretending to trip over in the streets. At that very moment, John suddenly stands up, cries out 'gotcha!' and walks away laughing, clearly unhurt. This new behaviour would lead me to conclude that I had made a mistake earlier in claiming that I knew that John was in pain. I might say to the passer-by: 'You were right: he wasn't hurt after all'. And I might even add, in a bid to apologize for my earlier rudeness: 'I'm sorry: I thought I *knew* that John was hurt. I didn't know he was just faking it'. My use of the verb 'to know' would, once more, be perfectly proper here: there is nothing in my use of the verb to suggest that I do not have mastery of it. What is more, I am using 'to know' in a situation where a mistake has occurred. In fact, it is precisely because a mistake has occurred that there is a purpose to my using this verb in the various ways that I do here.

According to Wittgenstein, looking at the way in which we use the verb 'to know' in ordinary situations helps to clarify its meaning. It does so because it helps to clarify what the *purpose* of the verb is. When we look at ordinary situations, we realize that the very purpose of our claims to know is to signal that we have a special kind of justification, special evidence or special grounds for our claim. And there is only a point in drawing someone else's attention to the special grounds that we have for our claim in situations where this claim could possibly be doubted and, therefore, possibly be mistaken. If doubt and error were genuinely inconceivable in an area, there would be no purpose in making knowledge claims in that area: there would be no point in drawing someone else's attention to the fact that one has a special justification, special grounds for one's claim.

This, of course, tallies with the example we have just been discussing. The passer-by's expression of doubt leads me to make my first knowledge claim and to justify it ('Look, I *know* that John is hurt: I just saw him trip over and now he's lying on the ground moaning'). In turn, the change in the evidence, when John stands up clearly unhurt, leads me to acknowledge my mistake and to change my knowledge claim ('You're right, he wasn't hurt after all. [. . .] I thought I *knew* that John was hurt. I didn't know he was just faking it'). It is precisely because doubt and error are possible in this area that there is a point in my making any knowledge claims at all and to provide grounds for them.

According to Wittgenstein, a survey of ordinary language shows that this is so in all areas that feature knowledge claims – not just in ordinary, everyday situations such as the one I have just described, but also in scientific language. Knowledge claims in the natural sciences (in medicine, biology, etc.) are made when special evidence has emerged in an area where error and doubt would be possible: 'we *now* know that this disease is not caused by lifestyle factors but that a virus is responsible for it'. These are also the areas were there is a purpose to putting forward justifications: 'we know that a virus is responsible, because we have tested and isolated it'.

For Wittgenstein, a survey of language (the language of everyday, ordinary situations, but also of scientific language) shows that the verb 'to know' is used in situations where doubt and error are possible and where there is therefore the need to justify our claims. The very purpose of saying 'I know that . . .' is indeed to *signal* that one has special grounds or special justification for a claim which could possibly be doubted or be mistaken. If doubt and error were not possible in an area, there would be no purpose in our justifying our claims or in our saying 'I know'.

This is Wittgenstein's first line of attack of the notion of private language. According to Descartes, I am only entitled to say that I know something if it is impossible for me to doubt or to be mistaken about that thing. Descartes also suggests that it is impossible for me to doubt or to be mistaken about my sensations, but that other people can be mistaken about them. Only I can therefore *know* that I am having certain sensations and what their nature is. If this Cartesian view were correct, a language whose words had my sensations as their meaning would be a language that only I could possibly understand. It would be a private language: only I could possibly know the meanings of the words in this language.

But Wittgenstein thinks that Descartes' conception of knowledge is ill-construed. He points out that knowledge claims only have a purpose, and therefore a place, in areas that allow for doubt and error. If it really were the case, as Descartes suggests, that I am infallible about my sensations, if this were an area in which doubts and mistakes are impossible, then this would be an area where knowledge claims would have no place. It would be improper for me to say 'I *know* that I am in pain'. In contrast, since other people can make mistakes and have doubts about my sensations, it would be perfectly legitimate for another person to say of me: 'I know that she is in pain'. There would be a genuine purpose to such a claim: in making it, this person would be signalling to others that they had special grounds for thinking that I was in pain. Wittgenstein's discussion of knowledge suggests that, if Descartes is right in saying that I am infallible about my sensations, then this has the reversed effect to the one Descartes was hoping for: if only I am infallible about my sensations, then it is not valid for me to say 'I know that I am in pain', but it is valid for others to say of me 'I know that she is in pain'. Wittgenstein writes:

Only I can know whether I am really in pain; another person can only surmise it. – In one way, this is wrong and in another it is nonsense. If we are using the word 'to know' as it is normally used (and how else are we to use it?), then other people very often know when I am in pain. Yes, but all the same not with the certainty with which I know it myself! – It can't be said of me at all (except perhaps as a joke) that I *know* I am in pain. (PI 246)

This is Wittgenstein's first line of attack on the notion of a private language. The idea of a private sensation language is based on the assumption that only I can know my own sensations, because only I am infallible about them. This assumption, however, is based on a misapprehension: for knowledge claims only have a place in those areas that allow for error and doubt. If it really were the case that I was infallible about my own sensations, then it would be improper for me to say 'I know that I am in pain', since I would thereby be attempting to shore up doubt in a matter which is *beyond* doubt. If, on the other hand, I am *fallible* about my own sensations, then I can, of course, say: 'I know that I am in pain'. In that case, however, I am in a similar position to other people making knowledge claims about my sensations. I can say 'I know that I am in pain', just as someone else can say of me 'I know that she is in pain': there is nothing special about my case. In this scenario, it would therefore be false to say that 'only I can know whether I am really in pain', since other people can also know this.

The point seems to turn, then, on whether I am infallible about my sensations or not. So a key question for us is: in Wittgenstein's view, am I or aren't I? Can I make a mistake about my own sensations?

This is a very tricky question. In order to try to address it, we need to revisit Wittgenstein's discussion of the role of ostension in the setting up of a private language. As we saw before, a private language is the one that is set up by carrying out internal ostensive gestures. Consider how a word might acquire meaning in such a language. The process would be as follows. I experience a sensation, I focus my attention inwardly on this sensation (as if I were pointing at it inside my mind) while repeating a word to myself – let us say the word 'S'. This process of focusing on my sensation while repeating a word gives my sensation a name, a label – the word 'S'. The process is thereby supposed to fix the meaning of the word 'S' (so that, thereafter, I can use the word correctly).

Let us examine this idea a little more closely. I repeat a word to myself while experiencing a sensation and this process, on its own, is meant to fix for me how the word should be used in a variety of future situations. According to Wittgenstein, there is a big problem with this approach to the setting up of sensation language. This approach presupposes that the nature of a sensation is clear to the person experiencing it – so clear, in fact, that having the sensation in and of itself gives one all that one needs in order to use the word correctly thereafter. So, my sensations, in and of themselves, dictate that it is appropriate for me to say 'I have a stabbing pain', but that it is not appropriate for me to say 'I have a square pain'. It is as if my sensations come to me perfectly delineated before I have the language to talk about them: their natures, how they differ from each other, all of these things are crystal clear before I have words for them. Indeed, acquiring a language about one's sensations is just a matter of attaching name labels to my sensations. Having attached these name labels, it is the very nature of my sensations (a nature that was clear to me before I developed this language) that dictates how these words are to be used.

Wittgenstein sees two major flaws here: first, inward ostension is not the kind of process that can give me the ability to use a word correctly; second, it is a mistake to think that the nature of sensations is clear to me before I develop language.

Let us consider the first point first. According to Wittgenstein, merely experiencing a sensation does not equip me with the ability to make the subtle, complex distinctions involved in using words correctly. Merely experiencing the sensation of pain does not teach me whether it is appropriate to say 'I have a stabbing pain' or 'My pain is square'. Instead, learning to use the word 'pain' involves being trained into a practice: a practice that rules out certain uses and allows certain others.

As for the second point, Wittgenstein suggests that it is a mistake to think of sensations as if their nature was clear to us before we have language. On the contrary, in his view, learning a language involves learning to categorize our sensations in particular ways. For instance, learning English involves learning to divide my pain sensations into throbbing pains, and stabbing pains, and dull pains. That pain can be divided into precisely these categories is not something that is crystal clear to me before I have language, simply from experiencing pain. It is something that I learn when I learn my language: when I learn to use my sensation words according to the established practice. At a more basic level, even, distinguishing between pain and other sensations (for instance, the sensation of hunger) is something that we learn when we learn a language. If a child says 'It hurts, I want to eat' and, having eaten, says 'It doesn't hurt any more', we would say to them: 'That's because you weren't hurting: you were *hungry*'. We all know that the sensation of hunger can be closely similar to that of pain. If our language happened to be different, we might not have ended up with a distinction between pain and hunger at all. But, our language does feature this distinction. When we learn it, we learn to divide sensations that can be quite similar into sensations of pain and sensations of hunger. Sensations are not things with natures that are perfectly clear to us before we have a language; rather we learn to divide sensations into different types of things with different natures when we learn a language, when we are trained into a practice of using words in particular ways.

In this respect therefore, it would be fair to say that, for Wittgenstein, I am not infallible about my sensations – certainly not in the pre-linguistic sense implicit in Descartes' view. I learn to categorize sensations when I learn a language, when I am trained into a particular practice. This training takes time. Before I master it completely, I might well find myself making the mistake of confusing pain with hunger or a dull pain with a throbbing pain. It is possible for me to make a mistake when I categorize a sensation: it is possible for me to be confused about its nature, just as it is possible for me to confuse a chestnut tree and a beech tree. I am not infallible about my own sensations.

In Summary

– The notion of private language is fuelled by the idea that only I have infallible knowledge about my sensations. However, a survey of language (of the way we use the verb 'to know' in ordinary situations and in scientific discourse) shows that knowledge claims have a purpose – and therefore a place – only in those areas that allow for error and doubt. Indeed, the purpose of making a knowledge claim (the purpose of saying 'I know that . . .') is to signal that one has a special justification, special grounds or special evidence for a claim that can be doubted and mistaken. If a claim could not be doubted or mistaken, there would be no point in doing this, and therefore there would be no point in using the verb 'to know'.

- The view that gives rise to the notion of private language turns on the idea that the nature of sensations, how they differ from each other, etc. are crystal clear to us before we have language. Indeed, in this view, acquiring a language about one's sensations is just a matter of attaching word labels to my – already crystal clear – sensations. Having attached these labels, it is the very nature of my sensations (a nature that was clear to me before I developed this language) that dictates how the words are to be used.
- For Wittgenstein, this view is flawed in two major ways: first, he suggests that this ostensive process (merely experiencing a sensation while repeating a word) does not equip us with the ability to use a word correctly in the required situations; second, he suggests that the nature of sensations is not clear to us before we acquire a language – rather, learning a language teaches us to categorize sensations in particular ways, to give importance to certain similarities and disregard others.

iv. CONCLUSION: PRIVATE LANGUAGE

In Wittgenstein's view, the notion of private language is deeply flawed. As we saw earlier, a private language is a language such that:

i. Words have as their meanings sensations that are private and transparent to the person experiencing it, that is: only this person can know the sensation directly (privacy); and only this person has infallible knowledge about the sensation (transparency).
ii. The person fixes and learns the meanings of these words by means of private, ostensive gestures.
iii. It is impossible for another person to understand this person's language.

For Wittgenstein, there are, at the heart of this notion of private language, two major confusions: that only I have infallible knowledge about my sensations; and that learning a sensation language is merely a process of attaching name labels to sensations whose nature is already crystal clear to me.

As soon as we consider how we use sensation words in language – as soon as we consider examples such as that of John pretending to be hurt or the kinds of conversations we have with children when we are teaching them about their sensations – we come to realize that both these points are mistaken. (It is perhaps no coincidence that, between writing the *Tractatus* and the *Investigations*, Wittgenstein spent several years teaching primary school children!) Knowledge claims only have a purpose – and therefore a place – in situations that allow for doubt and error: the claim that only I have infallible knowledge about my sensations is therefore flawed. And it is not the case that the nature of our sensations is clear to us before we learn a language: indeed, learning a language involves learning to divide our sensations into certain categories, it involves coming to regard certain similarities and differences between our sensations as important and others as negligible.

CONCLUSION TO PART II

The *Philosophical Investigations* marks a clear break from the *Tractatus*. At the same time, key aspects of Wittgenstein's philosophy remain similar throughout the two periods. In the *Investigations*, Wittgenstein continues to see his task as philosopher, first and foremost, as one of clarifying concepts – just as he did before. In his view, this task is important because the most apparently intractable problems of philosophy – such as those that emerge from the notion of a private language – are based on conceptual confusions.

Wittgenstein's philosophy, both in the *Tractatus* and in the *Investigations*, therefore has what we might call a strong therapeutic dimension: it aims to cure us of the philosophical ailments that arise from conceptual confusion and to give us the tools that might in future prevent us from becoming (philosophically) sick again. Perhaps ironically, for Wittgenstein this cure would ultimately consist in being able to stop doing philosophy altogether. He believed philosophy to be the single greatest generator of conceptual confusion; for this reason, he viewed most philosophy as intellectually dishonest and not part of a morally good life. It is perhaps not surprising, then, that whenever his students asked him about the possibility of pursuing a philosophical career he would try to discourage them, often nudging them instead towards professions involving manual work – which he regarded as intellectually more honest and, therefore, as more liable to make for a life of genuine moral worth. The idea that conceptual confusion is dishonest or ethically wrong and that conceptual clarity makes for a good life is, of course, one that was already part of Wittgenstein's thinking when he wrote the *Tractatus*.

Although Wittgenstein continued to pursue his philosophical work until the end of his life, he regarded his own case as exceptional.

When asked why he continued living in Cambridge and doing philosophy, rather than leaving philosophy altogether (as he suggested his students should do), he replied, semi-jokingly, that it was all right for him to do so because he 'manufactured his own oxygen'.[12] This reply may strike us as just a little disingenuous; a red flag certainly seems to go up when we hear the Cambridge don, ensconced in his cushy college, exhorting others to go out and pursue lives of potentially hard, unrewarding manual labour. But this does not really tally with what we know of Wittgenstein's life. He was certainly not shy of putting himself into situations of great suffering and hardship, as his experiences in the First World War should tell us; nor was he particularly drawn to the trappings of comfort, as is shown by the fact that he gave away his share of the family inheritance.

It is more likely that he genuinely believed himself to be more able to resist the philosophical pull towards conceptual confusion than others; perhaps that, having scrutinized it so closely and seen its pernicious effects at first-hand for so long, he was the ideal candidate for undertaking the difficult but necessary job of combating it. Having fallen foul, by his own admission, of conceptual confusion in the *Tractatus*, Wittgenstein believed that his later philosophical method – the method of observing how language is *used* ordinarily, the method captured in the injunction 'don't think, but look!' – was sufficiently important for him to remain (as it were) vigilantly at his task of showing philosophical problems for what he believed they were: pseudo-problems arising from confused concepts.

NOTES

1. Monk, R. *Wittgenstein: the Duty of Genius*, p. 271.
2. Monk, R. *Wittgenstein: the Duty of Genius*, p. 415.
3. The distinction between a proposition and a sentence (or propositional sign) and the role of use language also emerge quite clearly in TLP 3.11 and TLP 3.12, among others. However, in these remarks Wittgenstein is discussing the relation between propositions and *thoughts*, a subject we will only start to consider in Chapter 2.
4. Monk, R. *Wittgenstein: the Duty of Genius*, p. 118.
5. Monk, R. *Wittgenstein: the Duty of Genius*, p. 178.
6. Monk, R. *Wittgenstein: the Duty of Genius*, p. 178.
7. Monk, R. *Wittgenstein: the Duty of Genius*.
8. What, precisely, might be meant by 'me' here is of course an important question; one we will be touching upon again later.
9. On this period of Wittgenstein's life, see Monk, R. *Wittgenstein: the Duty of Genius*, part I, Chapters 6 and 7.
10. Note that this is conceptual, not causal necessity. Something is conceptually necessary if it is required by the concept. Causal necessity – the type of necessity we saw Wittgenstein reject in Chapter 3 – is supposed to hold between facts, not between concepts.
11. Wittgenstein deals with this issue in his 'Some Remarks on Logical Form'.
12. Lee, H. D. 'Wittgenstein 1921–1931' in *Philosophy*, Vol. 54, No. 208 (April 1979), pp. 211–220.

BIBLIOGRAPHY

PRIMARY TEXTS

Wittgenstein, L. (1929) 'Some remarks on logical form', *Proceedings of the Aristotelian Society*, 9 (Supplemental), 162–171.

Wittgenstein, L. (1958) *The Blue and Brown Books*, Oxford: Blackwell.

Wittgenstein, L. (1961) *Notebooks 1914–1916*, G. Von Wright and G. E. M. Anscombe (eds), Oxford: Blackwell.

Wittgenstein, L. (1961) *Tractatus Logico-Philosophicus*, D. F. Pears and B. F. McGuinness (trans.), London: Routledge.

Wittgenstein, L. (1965) 'A lecture on ethics', *The Philosophical Review*, 74 (1), 3–12.

Wittgenstein, L. (1967) *Zettel*, G. E. M. Anscombe and G. H. von Wright (eds), G. E. M. Anscombe (trans.), Oxford: Blackwell.

Wittgenstein, L. (1969) *On Certainty*, G. E. M. Anscombe and G. H. von Wright (eds), Oxford: Blackwell.

Wittgenstein, L. (1978) *Remarks on the Foundations of Mathematics*, 1956, G. H. von Wright, R. Rhees and G. E. M. Anscombe (eds), G. E. M. Anscombe (trans.), Oxford: Blackwell, revised edition.

Wittgenstein, L. (1980) *Remarks on the Philosophy of Psychology*, G. E. M. Anscombe and G. H. von Wright (eds), Oxford: Blackwell.

Wittgenstein, L. (1980) *Wittgenstein's Lectures, Cambridge 1930–1932*, D. Lee (ed.), Oxford: Blackwell.

Wittgenstein, L. (2001) *Philosophical Investigations*, G. E. M. Anscomb (trans.), Oxford: Blackwell.

SECONDARY TEXTS

Ahmed, A. (2010) *Wittgenstein's 'Philosophical Investigations': A Reader's Guide*, London: Continuum.

Anscombe, G. (1959) *An Introduction to Wittgenstein's Tractatus*, London: Hutchinson.

Baker, G. (2004) *Wittgenstein's Method: Neglected Aspects*, Oxford: Blackwell.

Canfield, J. (ed.) (1986) *The Philosophy of Wittgenstein: The Early Philosophy*, 15 volumes, New York: Garland.

Child, W. (1996) 'Solipsism and first person/third person asymmetries', *European Journal of Philosophy*, 4 (3), 137–154.

Child, W and Charles, D. (eds) (2001) *Wittgensteinian Themes: Essays in Honour of David Pears*, Oxford: Oxford University Press.

Crary. A. and Read, R. (eds) (2000) *The New Wittgenstein*, London: Routledge.

Diamond, C. (1991) *The Realistic Spirit*, Cambridge, MA: MIT.

Glock, H-J. (1996) *A Wittgenstein Dictionary*, Oxford: Blackwell.

Glock, H-J. (ed.) (2001) *Wittgenstein – A Critical Reader*, Oxford: Blackwell.

Glock, H-J. (2004) 'Was Wittgenstein an analytic philosopher?', *Metaphilosophy*, 35, 419–444.

Glock, H-J. (2006) 'Truth in the *Tractatus*', *Synthese*, 148, 345–368.

Hacker, P. (1986) *Insight and Illusion: Themes in the Philosophy of Wittgenstein*, Oxford: Oxford University Press.

Harcourt, E. (2001) 'Wittgenstein and "the Whereabouts of Pain"', in S. Schroeder (ed.), *Wittgenstein and Contemporary Philosophy of Mind*, Basingstoke: Palgrave, pp. 194–209.

Hintikka, M. and Hintikka, J. (1986) *Investigating Wittgenstein*, Oxford: Basil Blackwell.

Hyman, J. and Glock, H.-J. (eds) (2009), *Wittgenstein and Analytic Philosophy: Essays in honour of P.M.S. Hacker*, Oxford: Oxford University Press.

Ishiguro, H. (1969) 'Use and reference of names', in *Studies in the Philosophy of Wittgenstein*, G. Von Wright (ed.), London: Routledge and K. Paul, pp. 20–50.

Kremer, M. (2001) 'The purpose of Tractarian nonsense', *Noûs*, 35, 39–73.

Malcolm, N. (1984) *Ludwig Wittgenstein: a Memoir*, rev. ed. Oxford: Oxford University Press.

McGinn, M. (1997) *Routledge Philosophy Guidebook to Wittgenstein and the Philosophical Investigations*, Abingdon: Routledge.

McGinn, M. (1999) 'Between metaphysics and nonsense: the role of elucidation in Wittgenstein's *Tractatus*', *Philosophical Quarterly*, 491–513.

McGinn, M. (2001) 'Saying and showing and the continuity of Wittgenstein's thought', *The Harvard Review of Philosophy*, IX, 24–36.

McGinn, M. (2006) *Elucidating the Tractatus: Wittgenstein's Early Philosophy of Logic and Language*, Oxford: Oxford University Press.

McGinn, M. (2006) '"The Single Great Problem" Wittgenstein's Early Philosophy of Language and Logic', in *Wittgenstein: The Philosopher and His Works*, A. Pichler and S. Saatela (eds), 2nd Edition, Vienna: Ontos-Verlag, pp.107–140.

McGuinness, B. (1981) 'The so-called realism of Wittgenstein's Tractatus', in *Perspectives on the Philosophy of Wittgenstein*, I. Block (ed.), Oxford: Blackwell, pp. 60–73.

McGuinness, B. (2002) *Approaches to Wittgenstein: Collected Papers*, London and New York: Routledge.

McGuinness, B. (2005) *A Life: Young Ludwig, 1889–1921*, Oxford: Oxford University Press.

Monk, R. (1990) *Ludwig Wittgenstein: The Duty of Genius*, London: Jonathan Cape.

Moore, A. (2003) 'Ineffabililty and nonsense', *Proceedings of the Aristotelian Society* 76 (Supp.), 169–193.

Moyal-Sharrock, D. (2004) *The Third Wittgenstein: The Post-Investigations Works*, Aldershot, UK: Ashgate Wittgensteinian Studies.

Mulhall, S. (2006) *Wittgenstein's Private Language*, Oxford: Oxford University Press.

Pears, D. (1988) *The False Prison: A Study of the Development of Wittgenstein's Philosophy*, Oxford: Oxford University Press.

Preston, J. (ed.) (2008) *Wittgenstein and Reason*, Oxford: Blackwell.

Proops, I. (2001) 'The new Wittgenstein: a critique', *European Journal of Philosophy*, 9 (3), 375–404.

Schroeder, S. (ed.) (2001) *Wittgenstein and Contemporary Philosophy of Mind*, Basingstoke: Palgrave.

Schroeder, S. (2006) *Wittgenstein: The Way Out of the Fly-Bottle*, Cambridge: Polity Press.

Sullivan, P. (2002) 'On trying to be resolute: a response to Kremer on the *Tractatus*', *European Journal of Philosophy*, 10, 43–78.

Sullivan, P. (2003) 'Ineffabililty and nonsense', *Proceedings of the Aristotelian Society*, 76 (Suppl.), 195–223.

Sullivan, P. (2003) 'Simplicity and analysis in early Wittgenstein', *European Journal of Philosophy*, 11, 72–88.

Williams, B. (1981) 'Wittgenstein and idealism', in his *Moral Luck: Philosophical Papers 1973–1980*, Cambridge: Cambridge University Press, Chapter 12, pp. 144–163.

INDEX